DAY TRADING FOREX

This Book Includes- Day Trading Strategies, Forex Trading: A Beginner's Guide, Forex Trading: Proven Forex Trading Money Making Strategy - Just 30 Minutes A Day

BRANDEN LEE

CONTENTS

DAY TRADING STRATEGIES

Introduction	5
Chapter 1: How Day Trading Works	9
Chapter 2: The Personality of a Day Trader	17
Chapter 3: How to Manage Your Risks	21
Chapter 4: How to Find the Best Stocks to Trade	30
Chapter 5: The Tools and Platforms You Need	38
Chapter 6: The Candlestick Strategy	46
Chapter 7: The ABCD Pattern	55
Chapter 8: Reversal Trading	59
Chapter 9: Moving Average Trend Trading	67
Chapter 10: Resistance Trading	71
Chapter 11: Opening Range Breakout	77
Chapter 12: Red-to-Green Trading	83
Chapter 13: Some Other Strategies That Will Make You Successful	87
Chapter 14: Creating Your Own Day Trading Strategy	99
Chapter 15: Completing the Successful Trade	108
Chapter 16: Easy Day Trading Tips to Help You Succeed	119
Conclusion	129

FOREX TRADING

Introduction	135
Chapter 1: Forex Basics	137

Chapter 2: Advantages and Disadvantages of Forex Trading	169
Chapter 3: Forex Trading Broker	180
Chapter 4: Forex Trading Strategies	191
Chapter 5: Best Practices	213
Conclusion	229

FOREX TRADING

Introduction	235
Chapter 1: Forex Trading Basics	237
Chapter 2: Proper Money Management	250
Chapter 3: Cultivate a Forex Mindset	258
Chapter 4: Fundamental Analysis	268
Chapter 5: Technical Analysis	282
Chapter 6: Forex Strategy Basics	294
Chapter 7: Bollinger Band Bounce Trading Strategy	303
Chapter 8: Fibonacci Trading Strategy	313
Chapter 9: Bladerunner Trading Strategy	321
Chapter 10: Tips for Shortening Your Trading Work Week	332
Conclusion	346

DAY TRADING STRATEGIES

A Guide to Day Trading Strategies, Risk Management, and Trader Psychology

© Copyright 2017 by Lee Digital Ltd Liability Company All rights reserved.

The following eBook is reproduced below with the goal of providing information that is as accurate and reliable as possible. Regardless, purchasing this eBook can be seen as consent to the fact that both the publisher and the author of this book are in no way experts on the topics discussed within and that any recommendations or suggestions that are made herein are for entertainment purposes only. Professionals should be consulted as needed prior to undertaking any of the action endorsed herein.

This declaration is deemed fair and valid by both the American Bar Association and the Committee of Publishers Association and is legally binding throughout the United States.

Furthermore, the transmission, duplication or reproduction of any of the following work including specific information will be considered an illegal act irrespective of if it is done electronically or in print. This extends to creating a secondary or tertiary copy of the work or a recorded copy and is only allowed with express written consent from the Publisher. All additional rights reserved.

The information in the following pages is broadly considered to be a truthful and accurate account of facts and as such any inattention, use or misuse of the information in question by the reader will render any resulting actions solely under their purview. There are no scenarios in which the publisher or the original author of this work can be in any fashion deemed liable for any hardship or damages that may befall them after undertaking information described herein.

Additionally, the information in the following pages is intended only for informational purposes and should thus be thought of as universal. As befitting its nature, it is presented without assurance regarding its prolonged validity or interim quality. Trademarks that are mentioned are done without written consent and can in no way be considered an endorsement from the trademark holder.

INTRODUCTION

Congratulations on downloading this book and thank you for doing so.

The following chapters will discuss some of the basics that you need to know to get started with day trading. There are many different options that you can choose when it comes to picking out a good investment, and day trading can take you to the next level. There is some stress that comes with it, and you need to really understand the market, but that is where this guidebook can come in and help you to see success.

The beginning of this guidebook will spend some time discussing the basics that you need to know to get started with day trading. It will discuss the benefits of working with day trading, what day trading is and how it varies from other forms of trading in the stock market, how to pick out the right stocks to trade in, and even how to manage your risks. Before moving on, we will also talk about some of the tools and platforms that you need to have, such as picking out the right broker, to help you get a good start as a day trader.

In the second part of the guidebook, we will move on to some of the different strategies that you can choose to work with in day trading. There are many different trading strategies that are available, and each of them will have different rules and requirements that you need to follow to see some great results. And all of them can be successful as long as you learn how to use them properly. Some of the different day trading strategies that will be discussed inside this guidebook include opening range breakouts, reversal trading, ABCD pattern, resistance trading and so much more.

Getting started in day trading may not be the best choice for everyone, but for those who are ready to make good money in the stock market, for those who can keep up with the quick changes that come with day trading, and those who are ready for a great investment opportunity, day trading can be the best option. Make sure to read through this guidebook to learn all the tips and strategies that you need to be successful with your day trading investments.

There are plenty of books on this subject on the market, thanks again for choosing this one! Every effort was made to ensure it is full of as much useful information as possible, please enjoy!

CHAPTER 1: HOW DAY TRADING WORKS

Before you get started with your day trading adventure, it is important to know a little bit about the basics of day trading. Some people hear about this investment opportunity and how much money it can make them, so they jump in without doing any research. But this can be a dangerous way to do your work. It does not allow you to fully understand how day trading works and can even make it difficult to not lose money. Here we will look at some of the best strategies and tools that you can use to make you an expert when it comes to getting started with day trading.

Swing trading vs. day trading

What do you need to look for if you are a day trader? The answer is actually pretty simple in the beginning, but there are a lot of different parts that come with it. First, you want to take a look for stocks that have some movement, and you want this movement to be predictable. Second, you want to work with stocks that you can buy and sell on the same day. With day trading, you will never keep your position overnight and then sell the next day. If you do not make the trades on the same day, such as holding onto the stock overnight, you have switched from day trading to swing trading.

With swing trading, you are working with a type of trading where you will hold the stocks for a period of time. It is usually pretty short, and the trading will last from a day to a few weeks. The trading methods and strategies will be different for swing trading and day trading, so you should not use the same ones. They may seem similar because you are trading quickly in the market, but there are some key differences. Just remember, with day trading, you will purchase the stock and then sell it all on the same day.

This quick trading can be difficult for some people to deal with. If you are not careful with your selections, you may end up selling your stocks at the end of the day for a loss. But you really do need to let the stocks go, even at a small loss. If you hold onto the stocks overnight, the strategies for day trading may lead you to an even bigger loss the next day. If you want to be able to hold onto the stock for a few days and see if you can get a bigger profit rather than a loss, then you will want to go with swing trading instead.

Buying long and selling short

Day traders will always purchase a stock while hoping that the price will get higher. This strategy is known as *buying long*. Buying long will be a good option to go with any time you are looking at a stock, and you purchase it expecting that the price is going up.

That first part is pretty easy to understand, but what will happen if the prices of a stock start to drop? In this scenario, you can sell short, and you will end up making a profit in the process. It is possible to borrow shares from one of your brokers and then sell them, all while hoping that the price will get lower and that you will be able to purchase those shares at a lower price and make a profit. This is called selling short.

Let's look at an example of how this works. Let's say you borrow 100 shares of a stock from your broker and then you sell them at $100 a share. Then the price of that stock ends up dropping to $90. Now that the price has lowered, you will buy those shares back at the lower price and then give them back to the broker. You were then able to make $10 on each share, or $1000 total in this case. Of course, the market can also go up and then you will end up owing that money to your broker, so you really have to understand the market before you chose to go with this option.

This is why short selling can be a dangerous option to go with for beginners. It is hard to know when a share will go down and you could easily end up owing more money than you would make. Many beginners avoid this option, at least when they are first starting, to help them not get caught up and make the wrong decisions.

Institutional vs. retail traders

Individual traders are often known as retail traders. These people may work on trading either part-time or full-time, but they work for themselves and are not managing the money of other people. In reality, these retail traders are not a big part of the market because most people will trust a brokerage firm to help with their investments.

Then there are also the institutional traders which would include the big investment banks, trading firms, hedge funds, and mutual funds. These people are more professional with their trading and may use high-frequency trading or computer algorithms to help them get their results. These traders will often have a lot of money behind them, and they can add more aggressiveness to their trading than the retail traders.

As a retail trader, you may be curious as to how you will be able to compete against the institutional traders who have more money and more technology available to use. The biggest benefit of being a retail trader is that you can make choices about whether to stay out of the market or if you can trade at any given time. On the other hand, institutional traders will need to trade no matter what. As long as the retail trader does not get caught up with overtrading, they can use this to their advantage and make a great profit in the process.

Only trading the best

It is important that you learn what stocks are the best when you are a day trader. You only get one day to make a purchase of the stock and then sell it. You do not want to end up with a stock that quickly goes down and costs you a lot of money in the process.

This is why it is so important to come up with a strategy that will help you out. We will talk about a variety of strategies and methods that you can use to help you be more successful with your day trading.

The most important thing that you can do here though is to learn which stocks are the best. You need to be able to look at a stock and see whether it will continue to go up or not. Is this a good stock that has something unique about it, something that will keep it going up even if the market is going down a bit? Or is this a stock that is only going up because the whole market is seeing an upturn. This can make a big difference in which stocks you pick, and we will take some time to look at these and figure out which stocks work the best with the different strategies you will want to choose.

Advantages and Disadvantages of Day Trading

Pros

Making huge profit

With day trading, you can make a substantial profit. But of course, you can only achieve this if you have the traits of you true day trader – diligent, decisive, and responsible.

Boss spells Y-O-U

You are your own boss. As a day trader, you work independently. You can work at your most convenient time, take day offs if you want to, and work at your own pace.

Never gets boring

As a day trader, you need to work your wit every day against the market and other professionals – be it daytime or nighttime. Unlike the boring, trivial tasks in office or dull cold-calling, you, as a day trader, always feel the adrenaline rush every rapid-fire trading. Not because you want to, but because you need to. Especially if day trading is your primary source of income. Yes, in day trading, there will never be a dull moment.

Cons

You are your own boss

Being your own boss can be a very fun thing. But it's not always like that. Being your own boss (and focusing on day trading) means you need to quit your day job. That means giving up a stable, monthly paycheck. As a full-time day trader, you need to push yourself to work hard to earn enough profit to pay your bills and to enjoy a lifestyle you want.

Burn, baby, burn!

We're talking about getting burnt out in here. Day trading is not always rainbows and butterflies. There may be times when it feels like day trading is the worst storm in your life ever. Day trading can become very stressful because you need to monitor multiple screens to detect opportunities for trading. And when you find one, you need to act very quickly to exploit them. This is your everyday life as a day trader. Overworking yourself is mandatory in this kind of job.

CHAPTER 2: THE PERSONALITY OF A DAY TRADER

When it comes to day trading, there are some important personality traits that you need to possess if you would like to be successful. Not everyone will do well with day trading. It is a fast-paced world of investing, and you can quickly lose a lot of money in the process. And if you do not possess the right characteristics, you will find that you increase your risk of losing money more than before.

Before you decide to get into the world of day trading, you should consider whether you have the right personality to get started in this field. It can be tough for some people, but with the right personality traits, it will be a great option to help you make some money.

Some of the personality traits that you need to possess to do well with day trading include:

• Personal independence: this is a good work from home business. You need to enjoy the freedom of working on your own and not having someone looking over your shoulders all of the time. If you are not able to motivate yourself to get the work done or you thrive when you are in an office setting, you may find that it is difficult to get started in this kind of business.

• Decisiveness: when you are dealing with the market over the long term, you will notice that the market stays pretty steady. But when you work in the market on one day, there are a lot of ups and downs and the market may change on you in just a few seconds. Because of this, a day trader needs to be able to make quick and decisive decisions to keep them in the market. As a good day trader, you will need to rely on some of your past experiences to read what is going on with a new situation and make your decisions. There isn't a ton of room for second-guessing when it comes to day trading.

• Discipline and persistence: since you do not have a boss on your back when you work in day trading, you need to be able to keep yourself focused on the task at hand. You need to be able to watch the market, do your research, and be prepared to make the right decisions to make more money. And you need to realize that there will be a time when you are learning the ropes, and it may not be going the way that you would like. However, once you find a strategy that works for you and helps you to make a profit, then you will stick with it.

• Interest in trading: good traders will have some enthusiasm for the market for a long time before they decide to get into day trading. You should already have a natural inclination to follow commodities, bonds, stocks, and some of the other securities that are available. If you do not really have any interest in business or finances at all, then this will be a struggle to become a day trader.

• Personal support: you do need to have your own discipline and to be self-motivated, it is still nice to have some personal support along the day. The daily life of a day trader can be stressful and having some friends and family who will help you to keep in touch with the world can make a big difference.

• Financial independence: it is not a requirement to have a ton of money to get started with day trading. With that being said, you do need to have enough that you can do your chosen trades and then still have a little bit of a safety net in case the trades do not do that much. You should never trade with money that you cannot afford to lose. If you are someone who is living paycheck to paycheck, you need to take some time to build up savings before you even get started with day trading.

• Understand technology: all of your day trading will happen on your computer. If you do not have some familiarity with using a computer and with some of the platforms that are available, you will have a hard time working with day trading.

• Can keep your cool: there will be times, even with a good day trading strategy, when you make the wrong decisions, and your stocks will lose you money. If you are not able to keep your cool, you will end up making the situation a lot worse. You need to be able to look at the situation, whether you are earning money or losing money, and make good decisions that will help you to turn things around or to at least limit your losses.

There are a lot of different parts that come with becoming a day trader, and if you are not in the right frame of mind or do not have the personality for this, you will be disappointed with the lack of results that you will get. It takes a specific person to do day trading, and for those who do not have the right personality, it is best to pick out different investing options.

CHAPTER 3: HOW TO MANAGE YOUR RISKS

If you want to be successful at day trading, there are three things that you need to have. You need to have a sound psychology that can handle the stress of this trading style, a set of trading strategies that will help you make good decisions, and a good plan to help you manage your risk. If you are missing out on one of these parts, your whole program will fail, and you will not make money with day trading.

As a beginner, it is easy to focus only on the trading strategy that you are using. While the trading strategy is pretty important, it leaves you without the other three components that are just as important. Just because you have picked out a good strategy to work with does not mean you have the right self-discipline to stick with that strategy or to wait the market out long enough, and this could be the reason that you are failing, regardless of the strategy that you pick.

For this chapter, we will talk about risk management. There will be plenty of time for the strategies that you can use later, but for now, we need to learn some of the rules that you must follow to manage your risk. Of course, any strategy that you pick will have times when they will lead to a bad trade. The market does not always behave the way that it should or that we expect. But when you learn to manage your risk, you will not lose out as much money as you would just jumping into the market.

The first thing that you should do to manage your risks is to draw a line in the sand or have an exit point when you will decide it is time to get out of the trade. Pride can be hard to swallow for a lot of people, and they may find that it is hard to admit defeat or that they were wrong about a trade. But holding onto that trade will simply lead you to losing more money and will make the mistake bigger than before. You need to learn when to cut your losses and then walk away.

There will be times when the trade goes against you. This happens to beginners as well as to those who have been in the market for a long time. When the trade starts to go against you, it is time to exit. It is common in day trading for the unexpected to happen all of the time because there are such big fluctuations in the market from one moment to another. It may be hard to admit the defeat, but remember that there are always other trades that you can do on other days.

Your main job in day trading is to make money. If you are holding onto a position that is going against you just because you want to be able to prove that a prediction you made was right, then you are a bad trader. Your job here is not to always be right; it is to make money.

Another thing that you should do to minimize your risks is to always follow the plans and rules of your chosen strategy. This will be really easy when the trade is going well, and you are making money. But when you are in the middle of a bad trade, you may be tempted to go against those rules. This may seem like a good idea at the time, but it can end up costing you a lot of money. Following the rules of your strategy may make you lose a bit of money, but it is much easier to lose a little and get back into the game later than to end up with a big loss. It is better to take some of those quick losses, get out of the trade, and then come back to it all later on.

Next, you need to make sure that you are finding low-risk

entries that can provide you with a high potential reward. These can be risky still, but they pose a lot less risk than you will find with other stocks that you choose. The best setup is when you find an opportunity that will provide you with a trade that has a very little risk. For example, risking $100 to make $300 is a good setup, but if you are risking $100 to make $10, you are in the wrong trade. Most expert traders are not going to work on trades that have a ratio of less than 2 to 1 for profit-to-loss.

What this means is that if you purchase $1000 of stock and you are risking $100 on that stock, it is important that you sell that stock for a minimum of $1200 to make it worth your time and to decrease the risk. Of course, it may not always work out that way, and you may need to accept a loss, such as when the stock goes down to $900, but there should at least be the potential to make $1200. If the potential is only to make $1100 on the stocks, the profit-to-loss ratio is too low, and you should not risk it.

On some days, you are not going to be able to find a stock that has the right profit-to-loss ratio. That is fine. It is much better to stay out of the market for a day than to trade on a stock that does not provide the requirements that you need. You can enter the market later on, on another day or two down the line, knowing that you did not risk your money in the process. With the 2 to 1 ratio, you will be in a good position. Remember that there are still going to be times when you are wrong, or the market goes the opposite way than it should. If you stick with this ratio or better, you can still be wrong 40 percent of the time and make money from day trading.

The three questions to ask

Whenever you decide to purchase a stock on a trading platform, you are risking some of your money. Even stocks that fit into the ratio that we talked about before can run into some issues, and you have to realize that you are risking your money each time that you do this. However, there are some steps that you can take to manage this risk. The questions that you should ask yourself before any of your chosen trades include:

• Am I trading with the right stock: the first step of risk management is to work with the right stock? If you pick out the wrong stock, it does not matter what tools or platform you are using, you will end up losing. You need to make sure that you are avoiding stocks that do not have any movement, penny stocks that can be highly manipulated, ones that have a small trading volume, and those that are already being traded heavily by institutional traders and computers. We will discuss more about picking the right stocks to trade in a later chapter.

• What share size should I work with: the next question is to decide how many shares you should purchase. This will depend on how much money you have available and your daily goals. If you only want to hit a target of $1000 each day, then you will need to purchase more than 20 shares in most cases. If you do not have enough money in your account for this kind of target, then it is time to lower the daily goal.

• What is my stop loss: this is basically the amount that you are comfortable with losing if the market goes south. The most that you should never risk more than two percent of the equity in your account. This means if you have an account that holds $10,000, you should not risk over $200. This means that you may not make as much of a return on investment on your trades, but also helps you to keep most of your money in your account.

The three-step risk management plan

Step 1: the first step that you should take is to determine the absolute maximum dollar risk that you will take for the trade you are planning. It is recommended that as a beginner, you should never risk more than 2 percent of the equity in your account, but you can choose to go up and down from this number based on how much money you have and how much you are willing to risk. You need to have this amount calculated before you even start trading for the day.

Step 2: the second step is to estimate the maximum risk per share that you will take, the strategy stop loss, from your entry. We will learn more how to do this later because you will have a different stop loss based on the strategy that you choose.

Step 3: take the number from step 1 and divide it by the number you got from step two. This will give you the maximum number of shares that you can trade each time. Do not go about this level, or you are increasing your risk too much.

Let's take a look at how this would work. Let's say that you will get some stocks and you have $40,000 in your account. If you stick with the rule of only using 2 percent, then you would limit your risk to $800. We will be conservative for this trade as beginners and only risk 1 percent of the account, or $400. Now we have finished step one.

As you are monitoring the stock, you see that a situation is developing where you would use the VWAP Strategy (more on this later on) to get the best results. So you decide to sell the short stock when it reaches $50, and you want to cover them at $48.80, with a stop loss at $50.40. This means that you will be risking about $0.40 per share. This will be step 2.

Now we are moving on to step three. We will calculate our share size by dividing the numbers in step 1 and step 2, so we can find the maximum size that we can trade. For this example, we would be able to purchase a maximum of 1000 shares.

Now, with the money that you have in your account, you may not have the right buying power to get the shares at $50. So, you would choose to purchase fewer shares, such as 500 shares to get started with. With the strategies that we have talked about, you are never allowed to risk over 2 percent, but you can always be conservative and riskless.

Making sure you can handle the stress

And finally, to manage your risk, you need to make sure that you are actually able to handle the stress that comes from day trading. This is a stressful job. You are not able to just place your money on the market and then walk away from it, checking in on occasion. Rather, you need to be watching your stock the whole day. All those little fluctuations up and down can have a big impact on your potential earnings, and this can add a lot of stress to your day.

If you do not have the time to devote to this, at least on the days that you decide to trade, then this is not the right investment option for you. If you have trouble dealing with stress or you already have enough stress in your life, then day trading is not right for you. If you are not good at making decisions at the last minute and you let your emotions take over, then day trading is not for you.

Day trading can be a great investment option for you to work with, but you need to make sure that you are managing your risks and keeping them as small as possible. With the right strategy and risk management plan in place, even when you lose a little bit of money on an occasional bad trade, you will still be able to make a lot of money with day trading.

CHAPTER 4: HOW TO FIND THE BEST STOCKS TO TRADE

Once you have a good risk management plan in place, it is time to pick out the right stocks. You can have the right mentality and the perfect strategy, but if you frequently go into the market and pick out horrible stocks, nothing will save your trade. There are a lot of beginner traders who do not know how to find a good stock, or even what a good stock is all about. They will make a lot of mistakes and end up believing that this market is too hard to trade in. No matter what kind of trader you are, if your stocks do not have the right volume and they do not move, you will not be making money consistently. And when you trade in a stock that does not end up moving, it is basically a day that is wasted.

Of course, it is not just about the stocks moving; we actually want to see them move in a certain direction. We want to see them go up so that we can actually make a profit when we sell them at the end of the day.

Stocks in Play

One of the best options that you can go with is a Stock in Play. This is a stock that offers you a good risk to reward setup, which means that your downside will be 5c and your upside is 25c. These are nice because you can read these Stock in Play options that are about to switch around and will trade higher or lower from the present price. The moves on these stocks will be predictable, frequent, and you will be able to catch them before they make a change. They also allow you to be as efficient as possible with your buying power.

There are a lot of options when it comes to finding a Stocks in Play. Some of the things that they may be when you are looking for one includes:

• A stock that has some fresh news

• A stock that is up or down at least two percent before the market even opens.

- A stock that has a pre-market trading activity that is a little unusual.

- A stock that will develop important intraday levels which we can trade off from

You also want to make sure that you are picking out a stock that will do well, regardless of how the market is doing. There are some stocks that are simply going up because the rest of the market is going up. These are not the best stocks because they are also the ones that will go down as soon as the market goes down. Rather, you will want to go with a stock that does well no matter how the market does. These stocks will keep doing well, even with an economic downturn, and this makes them a great option to earn a profit.

Picking out a stock that has a good amount of liquidity is important as well. It is never a good idea to purchase a stock that you are not able to sell later on. When a stock is liquid, it means that there is plenty of demand with the stock and there are a lot of buyers and sellers. If you pick out a stock that is not considered liquid, which means that you will have a lot of trouble to sell that stock by the end of the day. But when a stock is liquid, you will not run into issues with selling them later on when it is time.

So, you may be interested in knowing a bit more about these Stock in Play options and what makes a stock fit in here. In many cases, this will be the new release of fundamental information about the stock, either during the same day you are trading, or the day before. This is why some of your research needs to include reading through newspapers and other sources to see what news or events are happening to different companies. This news can have either a positive or negative influence on a stock, and learning about it ahead of time can help you to either avoid or pick the stock, based on the information that you find.

There are a number of news events that you should look for to determine whether the stock will go the way that you would like. Some of these fundamental catalysts that can at least temporarily change the value of the stock include:

• The earnings reports of the company

• The pre-announcement of earnings

• Surprises in the earnings

• Disapprovals or approvals from the FDA concerning the stock

• Acquisitions or mergers of the company

• Alliances or major releases in products

- Major losses or wins with contracts
- Management changes, layoffs, and restructuring.
- Debt offerings, buybacks, and stock splits.

As part of your strategy, for pretty much all the different strategies that you choose, it is a good idea to spend some time checking the news and seeing what is going on with a company. Over time, you will be able to catch some of this news ahead of time, and then you can pick out a stock while the price is low, selling it later in the day when others hear the news and the demand go back up.

Float and market cap

There are three main categories that most stocks will fall into when it comes to retail trading. This type of categorizing will provide you with a bit more clarity on how to pick out the right stocks so that you can pick out a good strategy to go with them. First, we need to go through and understand some of the definitions that go with this part.

First is the float. Float means that number of shares that are currently available to be traded. This will vary based on how many shares the company offered out to stockholders to start with and how many shares the stockholders are willing to part with. There are some stocks, such as Apple, that are seen as mega-cap stocks that do not move much throughout the day because they need a lot of money and volume to be traded.

Then there are stocks that have what is considered a low float. This means that when a large demand comes around, it can quickly change the price of the stock. These are volatile stocks that move quickly, something that the day trader will really enjoy and since many of these low float stocks come in at under $10 (mainly because the companies that hold them are in the early stages and not that profitable), they can be easy for a beginner trader to come into. The hope with these stocks is that they will grow and the investor can make money.

So, back to the three categories that we just talked about. The first category will consist of the low float stocks, especially the ones that are priced at $10 or under. These stocks will be considered volatile, moving 10 percent or more each day. In fact, some of the more successful ones have been able to move over 1000 percent in one day. This can mean that you will make a good return on investment in this category, but it is important to be careful in this category. It is possible for you to turn a small investment into a large one with these stocks, but it is also possible to lose all your money too.

These stocks are often manipulated and can sometimes hard to trade with. Often experienced retail traders are the only ones who will trade in these stocks. This is where you will find the crazy claims of turning $1000 into $10,000 in one month, but it is hard to do, and most beginner and intermediate traders are not going to be able to do this efficiently. If you do decide to work with this kind of category, you should consider using the Bull Flag Momentum Strategy to see the best results.

The second category of stocks that you can consider is the medium float stock. The price of these is usually going to fall somewhere between $10 and $100. These stocks will often fall somewhere between 5 million to 500 million shares for the company, and many of the strategies that we will discuss later on will work well with these kinds of stocks. There are some options that will cost more than $100, but many traders will avoid these options. Since they are so expensive, you are not going to be able to purchase a ton of these options, and it makes them useless to day trade with those stocks.

The third category is the mega-cap stocks and would include

options like Apple and Microsoft. These companies will usually have more than $500 million public shares that can be available for trading. These stocks will be traded in millions of shares in a single day. These are the ones that will move only after the investment banks or institutional traders are selling or buying larger positions. A regular retail trader is not going to be able to move the price of the stocks.

In most cases, retail traders will not work with these stocks unless they can guess that a bigger institutional trader is about to make a big move that could benefit them. But unless you are sure about this, it is best to avoid working with these stocks because they are hard to deal with when you can only trade 100 to 1000 shares.

Finding the stocks that fit into these categories will be the biggest challenge that you will face when first getting started. You need to find a stock that will come in at a price that you can afford, one that looks like it will go up in price soon, and one that has enough volatility so that you can sell them (whether at a gain or a loss) at the end of the day. Following the tips in this chapter will ensure that you can get the right stocks and actually make a profit on most of the trades that you work with.

CHAPTER 5: THE TOOLS AND PLATFORMS YOU NEED

Like with any business you choose to go with, there will be some tools that you need to become a successful day trader. The most important tools that you will need are an order execution platform. And, if you are not already part of a trading community, you may need to have a stock scanner that will help you to find the best real-time setups that will make you money. Let's take a look to see what kinds of tools you need and how you can pick out the ones that are right for you.

Choosing your broker

When you first get started with day trading, especially when you are a beginner, you should find a good broker. Your broker will be the one who offers you advice on which stocks to go with and they will help you to make these orders at a good price and at the right time. There are a lot of different brokers out there, and picking out the right one will ensure that you will get the best results with your day trading. Pick out the wrong broker, and you will be disappointed.

The first decision that you need to make is the type of broker that you want to work with. There are some benefits to each one, and it often depends on how much you would like to spend, how much work you want the broker to do for you, and what features you would like them to offer to you. Some of the different types of brokers that you can choose from include:

• Interactive Brokers: The first type of broker that you can choose is an interactive broker. These brokers are pretty inexpensive and can cause you a $1 or less per trade. When you are purchasing 1000 shares or more, this is a pretty good price compared to the almost $5 or more that other brokers will charge you. Depending on where you live, they may also work with you without having to hold a large sum of money in the account ahead of time, making them easier to work with.

• SureTrader: This is a good option for those who are

international traders and those who fall below the $25,000 minimum that is a rule for U.S. residents who want to day trade. They will charge a bit more for commission though so be careful when you are choosing one. These companies will often charge you almost $10 for completing one buy and one sell. But if you are from the United States and you do not have $25,000 available to trade, this is one of the best options to go with because they do allow you to open an account for as low as $500.

Of course, there are many other types of brokers available. Some will offer you just advice to help you get started if you just want to do the work on your own. This can save you money, but remember that you are not going to get a lot of help in the process. On the other hand, you can also choose from a full-service broker who will not only offer you some advice but will be able to help complete the trades for you. It often depends on what you are looking for when it comes to your broker before you start.

One of the benefits of choosing a broker is that they will give you some leverage, about three to six times the leverage. This means that you may only put in $30,000 into the market, but you will have $120,000 in buying power (which means that you have a leverage of 4:1). This leverage is known as margin, and with many brokers, you can trade on the margin. This can help you out if you are short on money to get started, but you have to be responsible. Buying on the margin is easy, but it is also very easy to lose all of your money as well. The margin is good because it can give you the opportunity to purchase more than you could on your own, but it adds in more risk, and you may have to pay back more money than you can afford.

If you are using this leverage and then losing money, the broker will issue out a margin call. This is a serious warning, and it is best if you just avoid getting this at all. When you receive a margin call, it means that your loss is so much that it equals the original money that is in the account. If you do not add in some more money to the account, you will get a freeze on your account.

This is just one of the features that your broker may be able to offer you. Some will be able to offer platforms that are unique and will put you ahead of the rest of the game. Some will have different types of stocks that you can invest in and so on. It is a good idea to not only look at the fees that a particular broker is asking for their services, but also take a look at the different features and services that you would be able to get with them. You may be tempted to go with a cheaper option, but when you see all of the special features that another one offers compared to that cheaper option, it may be a better idea to spend a bit more.

Trading platform

As a day trader, you need to be able to complete your trades quickly, or you will not be successful. If you are working with a broker who does not use the right software or platforms, you may not get out of your trades fast enough, and you could end up losing money or missing out on a big profit. You do not want to be in the middle of a trade and see a big spike and then not be able to make changes or sell the stock because your platform is not the best.

There are many different trading platforms that you can work with. One option is known as DAS Trader, and it is really efficient when it comes to all of the things you need to do as a day trader. They have a helpful support team, and they are located near the NASDAQ data centers, so you are right in the middle of the market. There are many brokers that offer this platform when you are opening your account, while others will have their own platform.

The best thing that you can do is check out and see how

much you like the platform before you get started. Many brokers will have a trial run or a way to give the platform a try so that you can get familiar with how the buttons work and everything ahead of time. You may find that you like one platform better than another based on your own personal preferences. But no matter which platform you choose to go with, make sure that you are going with one that is quick, efficient, does not have a lot of down times and will make your day trading easier thane ver.

Real-time market data

With day trading, you need to be able to look at real-time data during the day. You do not get the benefit of waiting a few days or weeks for this data to come out because you need to enter and exit a trade in a short amount of time, sometimes within a few minutes of each other. There are some tools available for this, but remember that you will need to pay a fee for this, either to the platform you are using or to your broker.

Some people do like the idea of spending more money. They are already paying for their broker and some of the fees that are needed for their platform, and adding more seems like a waste. But depending on the market that you wish to trade in, you will find that having this real-time data will help you out a bit. It will help you to see what is going on in your market and can make it easier to adjust your trades, get out of the market when it is needed, and even to increase your profits.

There are a few different options that you can choose for this market data, but a good option to go with is the NASDAQ Total view level 2 data feed.

Joining a trading community

Day trading can be a very difficult thing to work on, and as a beginner, you may feel emotionally drained when you are done. And you are likely to have a lot of questions along the way. It is a good idea to join in a community of traders and talk to others who are in the same boat, asking questions as needed, to get the hang of things. It is normal to have some questions when starting out and joining one of these communities can make a big difference in how much you can do with day trading and whether or not you will be successful in the long run.

Having the right tools will make a big difference in how successful you can be with day trading. A good broker will be able to provide you with good advice and can even help to quickly do the trades for you. The right platform will ensure that you will be able to make the trades right when you need to. The right real-time scanner will let you catch some of the trends and keep up with how your stocks are doing. And a good community will be able to help answer any and all of the questions that you have along the way. Make sure that you have some of these tools, and you will be set to go.

CHAPTER 6: THE CANDLESTICK STRATEGY

Now that we have spent some time talking about day trading and how to get started, it is time to start talking about some of the strategies that you can use to become successful in day trading. Day trading is difficult, and if you do not take the time to pick a good strategy and learn it fully, it will become harder. The first strategy that we will take a look at is the candlestick strategy. There are a few options that come with it, and it often depends on which direction you think the market will go.

To create a candlestick chart, you need a few things. These things include:

• The opening price

• The highest price in your chosen time frame

• The lowest price that happens in that same time frame

• The closing price values for each time period that you want to show.

You can choose what time frame is used, but make sure that it is consistent for your whole chart. Some people go for the whole day, or you can choose an hour to help you out. the hollow or filled part of the chart will be the body while the thin lines that show up below and above the body will be the high and low ranges, and they are known as the shadows (or you can call them the tails or the wicks).

The high part will be marked by the top of the upper shadow

while the low by the bottom of the lower shadow. If the stock ends up closing higher than its opening price, you will then need to draw a hollow candlestick at the bottom of the body representing the opening price and the top of the body representing the closing price. On the other hand, if your stock ends up closing lower than it opened, the filled candlestick is drawn with the top of the body being the opening price and then the bottom being the closing price.

One thing to remember here is that the hollow candlesticks that have a close that is greater than the open will indicate that there is some buying pressure. However, if there is a filled candlestick where the close comes out as less than the open will indicate that there is some selling pressure.

Bullish Candlesticks

As mentioned, there are a few different types of candlesticks that you can work with, and the first option will be the bullish candlesticks. Candles that have a larger body towards the top are considered bullish, and they mean that the buyers will be the ones who are in control of the price. When you see this kind of chart, realize that it is likely that the buyers will keep pushing so that the price goes higher. This kind of candlestick is not only going to tell you the price, but it is also able to tell you that the bulls are winning and that they have the power.

Bearish candlesticks

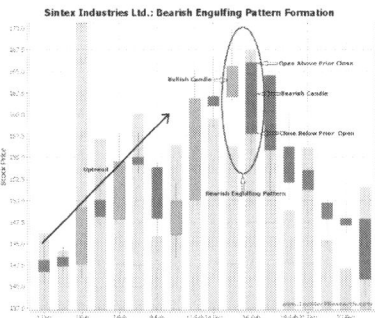

There are also the bearish candles. They will work a bit differently than you will find with the bullish candlesticks and can have you react in a different manner. When you see a bearish candle, it means that the sellers are the ones in control of the price action that goes on in the market and that buying would probably not be a good idea at this time.

When you see a candle that is filled and has a pretty long filled body, it means that your opening was high, but the closing was low. This is one way to tell that the market is bearish right now and it is probably not a good idea to get into the market at this time. You will probably not get a good price for the stocks because the market price is going down and there are not as many buyers interested right now.

Just by being able to read these candlesticks, you will be able to generate an opinion for how the stock will generally, or the price action. You need to understand which party (the buyer or the seller) is in charge of the price can help you determine whether now is a good time to purchase the stock or not. When you have a bullish market, the price will keep going up, so it is a good idea to jump in and then sell the stock at a higher price. But if you are in a bearish market, the price is most likely going to go down, and it is not in your best interest to make a purchase.

Indecision candlesticks

There are also some candlesticks that are known as indecision candlesticks. There are two main types of indecision candlesticks including spinning tops and Dojis. Let's take a look at these and determine what they both mean for the market.

Spinning tops

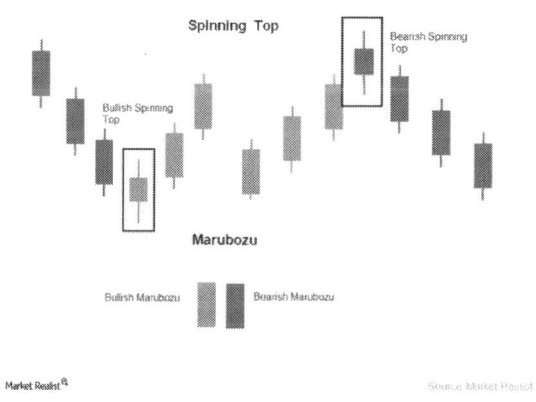

The spinning tops are candles that have the high wicks that are similarly sized and then low wicks that happen to be larger than the bottom and look a bit indecisive. With these candlesticks, the sellers and the buyers have powers that are pretty close to even. No one is really in control over the price of the stock, but there is still a fight that is going on. The volume on these will be lower because the traders want to wait and see whether the buyers or the sellers will be the ones that wend.

You will notice that a trend in the price is often going to change right away after this kind of indecision candle, once the fight has been won by either the sellers or the buyers, so it is worth your time to recognize this kind of price action. You may want to wait a bit before jumping into the market to see which way the market will go. Sometimes it will go well, and the price will go up, but the market could also go the other way, and you could see the price drop.

Dojis

Another type of candlestick pattern that you should watch out for is the Doji. There are actually a few forms and shapes of this, but they are either going to have no body to the candlestick or at least a really small body. When you see that there is a Doji in the chart, it means that there is a fight that is going on between the bulls and the bears and no one is winning yet.

There are some times when the Doji will have a bottom and top wick that are unequal. If the top of the wick ends up being longer, it means that the buyer tried to get the price higher, but they were unsuccessful. They may show that the buyers are starting to lose power and it is possible that the sellers may start to take over. On the other hand, if the bottom wick is longer, this means that the sellers tried to push the price down and they were not successful. This may mean that there will be a takeover of the price action by the bulls.

You can definitely use this to help you see what trends are going on. If one of these candlesticks shows up during a bullish trend, it means that the bulls are wearing out and now the bears are trying to take over control of the price. If this candlestick forms when there is a bearish downward trend, it suggests that now the bears are tired and now the buyers or the bulls will take over the price. This can help you to see when a trend is about to occur in the market and can help you to make some smart decisions.

The candlestick pattern is a great way to predict how the market is going. When the market is going up based on these candlesticks, you will want to purchase and then sell before they go down. When the market is going down based on these candlesticks, you will either want to stay out of the market if you are not already in, or you will want to sell before the price goes down and you lose too much money. Take some time to learn how to make these charts, and you will find that they are a fantastic way for you to monitor the way that the market is going.

CHAPTER 7: THE ABCD PATTERN

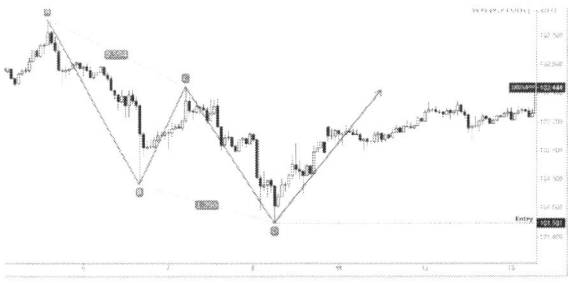

As a beginner trader, you may want to consider working with the ABCD pattern because it is basic and easy to trade with. Although it has been around for some time and it is simple, it is still effective, which is why so many traders are still using it. With this strategy, you will do whatever the other traders in the market are doing because you believe that the trend is your friend. Let's take a look at how this one can work.

The ABCD pattern will start out with an upward move that is strong. At this time, the buyers are aggressively buying a stock from point A and making constantly new highs of the day, which is point B. You will want to get into the trade at this point, but do not chase the trade since point B is already an unusually high price. Plus, at this point, you are not able to say where the stop loss should be and it is never a good idea to trade without setting the stop point.

At point B, the traders who already bought the stock at an earlier time will start to slowly sell their stocks to make some profit, and this will get the price to come down. It is not a good idea to enter into a trade at this time because you will not be able to guess where the pullback will happen. However, if you see that the price isn't coming down from a specific level, such as point C, this means that the stock is working with some potential support. This means that you will be able to plan the trade and then set up the stops that you need so that you make the most profit.

This strategy is pretty basic and can help you to get the results that you would like out of your trading strategy. Let's take a look at some of the steps that you would do with this strategy so that you can start to use it for your own personal gain with day trading.

• When you are looking at your scanner that there is a stock that is surging up from its point A and it has reached a new big high for the day, which is point B, you should take a look. You will want to look to see if the price can make a support that is higher than point A. If it does get that support, that will be your point C. Just make sure that you are not jumping into this trade too early.

• Then you will want to make sure that you are watching the stock at least through the consolidation period. From this information, you will be able to choose the share size that you want to work with as well as the exit and stop strategy.

• When you start to notice that the price is holding support at point C, it is time to enter into the trade at a price that is as close to point C as possible. The anticipation is that it will move up to point D, if not higher.

• For this option, the stop will be the loss of point C. If at any time of the day, the price ends up going lower than point C, it is time to sell the stock and accept the loss that you have. This is why it is so important to purchase the stock close to point C so that you can keep your losses to a minimum.

• If the price of that particular stock continues to go higher, it is time to sell half of your position when it reaches point D. You can then bring the stop higher to the entry point so that you at least break even.

• As soon as the target is hit or you start to see that the price is losing some steam, it is time to sell the rest of your shares. When the price ends up getting to a new low, it means that the buyers are getting exhausted and the trend will move backward.

As you can see, this is a pretty basic strategy that you can use, and as long as you wait to enter the market until a good point is reached and you stick with your stop points, you will make a profit from it. You do need to watch the stock though because it is possible for the trend to turn too much. And do not purchase the stock too far from point C, or you will miss out on some of the profits that you can use. If you are a beginner and want a chance to get into the market and see how day trading works without having to get into the harder strategies, then the ABCD strategy is a good one to work with.

CHAPTER 8: REVERSAL TRADING

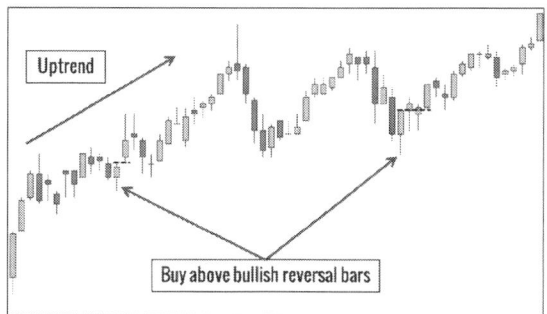

The bottom and top reversal options are two trading strategies that a lot of day traders will rely on. This is because the reversal strategies will have defined exit and entry points, which gives you some clear guidelines about when you should get into the market and when you should leave the market. You will be able to find the best reversal setups using a scanner and indecision candlesticks will help you to set up your entry points and more so that you get the best results with the reversal trading.

When you are working with a reversal strategy, you will notice that there are four important elements that need to be present. These four elements include:

1. There needs to be a minimum of five candlesticks present on a five-minute chart. They can be moving downward or upward, but they need to be present.

2. The stock will have an extreme five-minute Relative Strength Index indicator. If the RSI is above 90 or above 10, it should catch your interest. This RSI will compare the magnitude of recent losses or gains over a specified period of time to measure how fast and how much the price movement was. The values will be on a range from 0 to 100. This can be used to help you recognize a stock that is oversold or overbought. If the RSI is over 90, it shows that the conditions of the stock are overbought and if the RSI is below 10, it means that the conditions are oversold.

3. The stock is being traded near, or at least close, to an important support or resistant level.

4. Once you are seeing a trend that is coming near an end (which can be seen with indecision candles), you could be near

a reversal. This is what you should be watching out for, and you need to be ready.

When you work with reversal trading, you will look for an indecision candlestick. These are important because they will indicate that a current trend will change soon. The Doji candlestick will really help to show this. For example, if you have a candle that has a top tail, you can figure out that during this period, the price went up, but the market was not able to hold at this level, so the stock was sold off. It will depict the battle where the buyer lost their push up. Soon the seller will be able to control the price, and this will push it back down.

This can be true going the other way as well. When the candle has a long lower wick, you will be able to guess that at some point during this period, the price moved down, was not able to hold at these levels, and then was bought up. With this battle, the sellers lost with their push down, and it is likely that the buyers will push the price back up again.

During a reversal trading strategy, you will want to look for these indecision candlesticks because they will show that the current trade will change soon. You want to make sure that what you are showing is clearly going to be a reverse because it is never a good idea to be on the wrong side of the next reversal trade. This means that when a stock is not selling well, you do not want to make a purchase assuming that it will buy back up. When the stocks are dropping, it is best to wait until you can confirm that there is a reversal. A good way to see this is when you see that a Doji or indecision candle is forming.

You can also look at the RSI to see if it is above 90 or below 10. When you see this, you will want to look for the actual entry near a strong intraday support (if you are working with a bottom reversal), or a resistance level (if you are working for a top reversal).

Let's take a look at the bottom reversal first. In this one, when you have a long line of candles next to each other that are making new lows, the first candle that shows up that makes a new high near an important support level will be the most important. For many traders, this will be the entry point. You will still be able to get the stock for a low price due to the history of it, but since there was one candlestick that went up, it is likely that the trend will change and you could sell at a much higher price when the trend reverses.

Once you are working with one of these bottom trades, your

exit indicators will be pretty simple. If the stock goes up and then moves back down, it is a good idea to stop out and take a loss. If you purchase the stock hoping that it will go higher and the price goes sideways, this is a sign that the price will go down again and will keep on dropping, so it is best to get out of the market. If you get into the market and the price stays flat for even a few minutes, it is time to get out, regardless of what happens next. And then if the price goes up, you know that you will make a profit and can watch out for some of the other indicators for when you should get out to still make a profit.

In reversal strategies, one of the biggest things that you need to do is watch the stocks that are going up or down, while also looking for possible resistant and support levels and areas that will result in a good opportunity to trade. This is a good idea because it makes it harder to be impulsive and reduces the amount of times that you rush into the trade. Rather, you should always wait for times when there is stagnation in the market before joining into the trade.

To summarize the strategy that you need to use for the bottom reversal strategy includes:

- Set up a scanner that will let you know when four or more

candlesticks start to go downward extremely. You can then take a look at this stock and review the daily levels of support and resistance near the stock to see if it will be any good.

• You need to wait for the confirmation of a few things. First, you want to have the formation of a bullish Doji or at least an indecision candle. Then you want to make sure that the stock is being traded near or at a significant intraday support level. And finally, you want the RSI to be lower than 10.

• You will continue to watch the stock, and when it makes a new high at 1 or 5-minutes, it is time to buy the stock.

• The stop loss will be the low of the previous red candle or at least the low of the day.

• The profit target for this is either going to be the next level of support, the Volume Weighted Average price, or the stock reaches a new low at the five-minute, which shows that the seller is starting to gain control again.

You can also choose to work with the top reversal. This strategy will be similar to what you can find with the bottom reversal option, but you will work on the short selling side. The steps that you need to follow to make this one work well for you include:

Set up a scanner that will highlight any stock that has at least four candlesticks next to each other that are moving up. When this hits the scanner, take a look at the daily level and the volume of your resistance and support near the stock to see if it will work.

- You will then want to wait for a confirmation of the top reversal strategy. This can include the formation of a bearish indecision candle, the stock being traded near an important resistance level, or it has an RSI that is more than 90.

- When the stock reaches a new low at the five-minute part, this shows that there is a sign of weakness. It is time to short sell the stocks that you already own if you have some shares available.

- The stop for this will be the high of the previous candlestick, or you can go with the high of the day.

- The profit target will either be when the stock makes a new five-minute high or when it reaches a new support level.

There are some day traders that will base their whole strategy on using reversal trades, and they can be very successful with them. These strategies are pretty secure, once you learn how to use them and they have a risk to reward ratio that is good. Plus, each day that you use this strategy you are sure to find some stocks that will work well for these trades. If you are uncertain about what kind of trading to go with on a particular day, it may be time to consider working with a reversal strategy and seeing how it works for your needs.

CHAPTER 9: MOVING AVERAGE TREND TRADING

The next strategy that we will take a look at is the moving average trend trading. There are some traders who will use the moving averages as a way to pick out a potential entry and exit points for the stocks they are trading. There are many stocks that will start with an upside or a downside trend once they have started their morning trend and you will be able to see their moving averages in the 1-minute and 5-minute charts as a type of moving resistance or support line. This can be a benefit for you because you can ride the trend with the moving average.

The moving average trend will sound complicated to work with, but the steps are pretty simple to work with and include:

• When you are looking at a Stock in Play, and you see that there is a trend that is starting to form around a moving average, it is time to consider trend trading. You will want to take a look at the stocks' trading data from the day before to see how the stock responded to those moving averages.

• Once you see which moving average is the most suitable to the behavior of your trade, it is time to buy the stock. Of course, you should wait to confirm the moving average is the support and you always purchase close to the moving average line as you can. Picking out the stop is pretty simple. You should place the stop about five to ten cents below this moving average line. If you are using a candlestick chart, you will want to place the start close to the moving average for the long positions.

- Now you will just ride this trend until the moving average breaks.

- It is never a good idea to use trailing stops with this option, and this strategy will require your full attention. Use your own eyes, and not some scanner or other tools to monitor how the trend is doing.

- If the stock starts to move really high from your moving average, this means that you are making a nice profit. It is sometimes a good idea to take your half-position rather than going all the way to the break. This is at least going to provide you a profit, and sometimes the moving trend will go down before your break. If this happens, you could lose out on all of the profit. If you sell at your half=position, at last, you made some profit.

This is a strategy that some traders like to do, but many beginners will avoid because it leaves you exposed to the market for a longer period of time. Some of these trending trades can last for a few hours or more, and for some day traders, this is just too long to trust the market. Most day traders like to go much faster, getting the profit in a few minutes, but if you are interested in trading over a few hours, it could be the best option for you.

Some beginners like this option because it helps them to get familiar with the trading and it does not require decision making that is quite as fast as the other options. You also will not have to rely on Hotkeys when starting. You can use the trending strategy to recognize your stop loss and your entry points easier than some of the other methods as well, something that is especially important for those traders who are stuck paying higher retail commissions and who are not able to get in and out of their trades without paying a big fee. Since the moving average trend strategy has an exit and entry point that are easy to see, it is easier to get a good profit with only two orders, which can save some traders money.

CHAPTER 10: RESISTANCE TRADING

Support and resistance trading are really popular, and you will probably find a lot of traders who decide to go with this kind of strategy to help them do well. In these cases, support will be the price level when buying is so strong that it can reverse or interrupt the current downtrend that is going on. When your current downtrend ends up hitting a new support level, it will bounce. The support will then be shown on a chart using a horizontal line that will connect at least two bottoms.

On the other hand, the resistance will be the opposite. This is the price level where the selling position is so strong that it can reverse or interrupt the uptrend. When your uptrend hits that resistance level, the trend will stop and sometimes it will even tumble down. Resistance can be represented on your chart by a horizontal line that will connect at least two tops.

It is possible to get minor resistance or support. These will cause the trend to pause. But when you are working with a support or a resistance that is considered major, it can make the trend reverse. Traders who use this strategy will buy at the support and then sell at the resistance, often causing the strategy to be more effective because of the way they are behaving.

Finding the resistant or support lines on your daily charts can be difficult, and there will be some times when it is hard to draw a line that is clear. You do not have to draw anything on the chart if you cannot find it that day because if you are missing out on the line, it is likely that others would not see them either. When this happens, you may want to consider another strategy for the day.

When you are ready to draw some of your own resistant or support lines on your daily charts, here are some of the tips that you can use to make it easier:

• You will usually start to see indecision candles in the area of resistance or support because this is where the sellers and the buyers are closely fighting against each other.

• It is common to see whole dollars, and half-dollars will act as the resistance or support level, especially when you are working with stocks that are $10 or less. If you are not able to find the resistance or support line that is near these numbers on your daily chart, remember that these numbers can be like an invisible line.

• When you are drawing the lines, you need to make sure that you are looking at data that is recent to get the best results.

• The more of the line that touches onto an extreme price, the more that the line is a good option for your resistance or your support and it will have some more value. You will really want to emphasize this type of line.

- You only want to consider the resistance or support lines that are in the current price range. So if the price of the stock is at $20 right now, it is not worth your time to look for these lines in the region of when the stock was $40. It is not that likely that the stock will get up to that area again so stick with the range where it is right now.

- Remember that these lines are not going to be an exact number and they are more of an area. So, if you find an area that is around $19.69 for a support line, you will see the movement to be near that number, but not exactly that number. It is usually fine to see the area being between five to ten cents of the number that you find.

- The price that you are working with needs to have a clear bounce from that level. If you cannot determine if the price has bounced at that level, it is probably not the resistance or support level that you want. Resistance or support levels that are important will stand out and be really noticeable, so if you are questioning one of them, they are not the right one.

- When it comes to day trading, it is best to draw these lines across the extreme prices on daily levels rather than across any areas where many of these bars have stopped.

When you first get started with these lines, you will find that drawing them will be pretty tricky. The good news is that when you get started and try it a few times, you will get the hang of it and see that it is not too hard.

Once you have been able to draw these resistance and support lines, it is time to work on this strategy to decide when it is time to purchase and sell the stocks that you are working with. To get started with this trading strategy, follow these easy steps to help you get started.

• In the morning, make your watchlist for the day. Look at the charts and then use the steps above to pick out your areas of resistance and support.

• Now watch the price action in those areas on your five-minute char. If you find that an indecision candle is forming near that area, it is a good confirmation of that area, and you can enter the trade. You will want to make a purchase as close to the support level as possible because this will help you to minimize your risk.

• You will then decide to withdraw and take out a profit when you reach the next support or the next resistance level.

• You will want to keep the trade open so that you can hit your target for profit or until you reach a new resistance or support level.

• Some traders will sell at half-positions near the profit target before moving the stop up to the entry point to break-even.

• If you are looking at the charts and there are no obvious resistance or support levels that you can work with next, it is time to consider closing your trade. It is best to do this at the nearest round-dollar or half-dollar levels.

There are a lot of stocks that will work with this kind of trading, and it can be a great one to help you to figure out the best time to enter the market and when to end. You will need to have some practice on how to draw your own resistance and support lines, but once you have that part down, it is really easy to work with this kind of strategy to see results.

CHAPTER 11: OPENING RANGE BREAKOUT

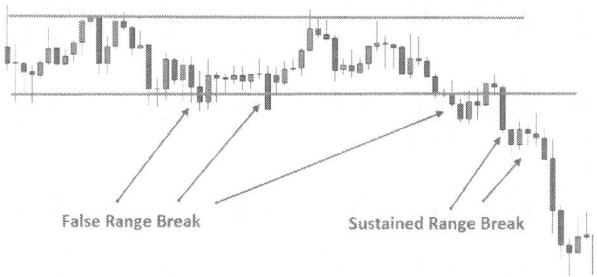

Now we will take a look at another trading strategy that is pretty well known and it is called the opening range breakout, or ORB, strategy. This is a good strategy because it will signal an entry point, but it does not tell you the profit target. You will be able to pick out the best target for the profit based on some of the other strategies that we have talked about in this guidebook or by looking at some of the charts that are available.

The ORB will be used as an entry signal only, but to finish the trade properly, you need to make sure that you also define the stop loss the exit, and the proper entry as well.

Right when the markets open, you will notice that the Stocks in Play will experience a very violent price action because of all the buy and sell orders that flood into the market right away in the morning. This trading will usually show up during the five minutes of the market day because o the loss or the profit that occurred for people who held their positions overnight. There are also going to be a lot of new traders and investors who want to get into the market and will want to do so right away in the morning.

There are some investors who will see that their position went down during the night and they will panic so they will sell off their stocks. There are also a lot of new investors who will see that a stock is low in price and will jump in right in the morning before the price goes up. Both of these will determine the price of the stocks and how they will do during the day.

As an investor, you will want to give this opening range a minimum of five minutes before you choose to invest. It is hard to figure out whether the buyers or the sellers will win out in the market when there is so much change going on in the market. It is best to wait at least five minutes before you make any trades with this strategy, but there are some traders who will wait up to an hour so that they have a better chance at identifying the balance of power that is available between the sellers and buyers.

Once the opening is done, the trader can work on their trade plan based on the thirty or sixty-minute breakout. There are some that will do even smaller time frames than this, such as a fifteen-minute breakout. The longer the time frame that you do with this, the less volatility that you will be able to find in the market and it will change what you are doing.

Just like with many of the setups that you are working with, this ORB strategy will work the best with either large or mid-cap stocks, ones that are not going to have big price swings throughout the day. You do not want to go with this strategy when you have low float stocks. If possible, you will want to pick out a stock that will be able to trade inside a range that is smaller than the ATR, or the Average True Range, of this stock. You will be able to figure out this number by looking at the highs and lows of your candlesticks.

To work with the Opening Range Breakout Strategy, you will want to use the following steps:

• After you have created your watchlist early in the morning, it is time to monitor the stocks for at least the first five minutes of the market opening. You should identify their price action and the opening range. Look to see how many of the shares are being traded at that time and determine if the stock is going up or down. Are there a lot of orders that are going through here or is there a high volume that has just a few large orders with it? It is important to look at the numbers of orders that are being sent in because this really shows how liquid the stock is.

• You need to make sure that you can determine what the ATR is. In this step, you want to make sure that the opening range is much smaller than the ATR so keep that number on hand.

• After the first five minutes of the market are done, you may notice that the stock may still be traded in that opening range for a little bit longer. However, if you notice that the stock starts to break out of the opening range, it is time to enter into the trade. You will want to enter into the trade going in the direction of the breakout. You will want to go long for a breakout that is upward, and you will want to go short for a move that is downward.

• You will want to do the stop loss below the VWAP for your long position and then have a break above the VWAP for a short position.

• You will want to make sure that you pick out a good profit target as well. You will first need to take a look at the daily levels throughout the day and then identify it in the pre-market. You can also look at the close from the previous day and the moving averages that are on your daily chart.

• If there isn't a good technical level for your profit target and your exit, you will want to look for some signs of weakness in the stock, if you are long. If you are doing a short position, you will want to exit when there is a strength in the stock. For example, if the price reaches a new low, this means that it is reaching a weakness and if you are long, you will want to look at selling your stock. If you take a short position and the stock gets to a new high, then it is a good sign o a strength, and you may want to cover that position to help you out.

This is an example for working with five minutes ORB, but it is possible to use the same ideas when you are working with fifteen or thirty-minute opening range breakouts depending on what you want to do with the market.

This is a great option to go with that will ensure that you are not going to be fooled by the changes that occur right at the beginning of the market, but you can still get a good look at how the market will go for the day. Make sure that with the ORB, you are not supposed to trade during the first five minutes or more in the morning because the whole market is just too volatile, but you can still use this information to help you get started on the right foot and can give you a way to make a lot of money with your trading strategy.

CHAPTER 12: RED-TO-GREEN TRADING

If you are looking for another easy to work with trading strategies, the red to green option is a good one to work with. This one will rely on the information from the previous day close to help you figure out where the stock will go and what decisions you need to make.

While looking at this information, if you notice that the current price of the stock is higher than it was on the previous stay, this means that the market is moving from what is called a green day to a red day. This means that the percentage that the price has changed will now be negative, which will be shown as red in most of the platforms that you look at. This is known as a green to red move.

On the other hand, if the price is lower than what you found on the previous day, this means that the market is moving from a red day to a green day. This means that the percentage that the price has changed will be positive now, which will be shown as green in color on most platforms. This will be considered a red to green move.

You will find that this will be a strategy that is pretty much the same whether you are working with green to red and for red to green, except for the direction that the trade is going or whether it is long or short. So, to keep things simple here, we will just stick with one of them and use the same rules for both of them.

To summarize the strategy that you would like to use with trading the red to green strategy, you would go with the following steps:

• When you are creating your watchlist for the day, you will want to take a look at the previous day close and then monitor the price action at that time.

• If you see that the stock is moving towards where it was at the previous day close with a high volume, it is time to consider going long, using the profit target that occurred on the close of the previous day.

• The stop loss that you will use will be the nearest technical level. This means that if you buy near the VWAP, the stop loss will be when there is a break of the VWAP. If you are buying near a moving average or an important support level, you will want to place the stop loss near the break of the support level or the moving average.

• It is a good idea to sell at the profit target. If the price ends up moving in your favor, it is time to consider bringing the stop loss up the break-even point and then make sure to not let this price go against you. When you are done with that, the red to green move should start working right away.

You will be able to use an approach in a similar way if you want to work on the green to red strategy because they work pretty much the same way.

CHAPTER 13: SOME OTHER STRATEGIES THAT WILL MAKE YOU SUCCESSFUL

So far this guidebook has spent quite a bit of time talking about a lot of great day trading strategies that you can work with. Each of them is an easy strategy that will help the trader get started, as long as they can pick out the stock that works the best for that strategy. You will be able to see success with any of the strategies that we have talked about so far in this guidebook, but you need to learn all of the requirements of that trading strategy and stick with it no matter what. If you can do that, without switching between one strategy and another, you are more likely to see some great results in no time.

Gap up, inside bar, breakout strategy

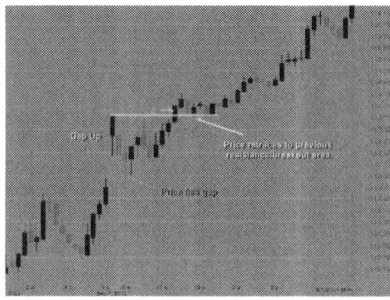

This kind of trading signal will start with a gap up. If the second or third ten-minute bar then develops to be an inside bar, then you know that you have the setup that you want.

Some traders decide to go with an alternative that includes stocks that have just a partial gapped up, but only do this if they are listed high on the gainer's list. When we are talking about a bar that is partially gapped up, we are talking about the setup having a gap that is higher than it was at close the previous day, but it still comes in below the high of the previous day. This type is still able to provide you with some good signals for the day, especially if you are low on stocks that have the full gap.

With this method, it is best to go with only one or two of those ten-minute bars develop before you get the inside bar. If there are more than these two, it means that the price has already had too much movement and this is not going to be an effective setup. Once you have that inside bar, it is time to place a buy stop that is right above the high that is inside that bar. The trigger is the breakout above the inside bar.

From this point, you will wait to find when the trade signal is leaving you long. Then if you have the stop in place, it is time to think about where and how you want to exit from the trade. If your stop is hit in this trade, you will just count it as a loss, get out of the trade, and then move on to trying something else.

Gap up, attempt to fill, breakout

This is a great strategy to go with as a beginner because it is so simple and it uses a lot of common sense to help get the work done. As the name suggests, you will be looking for a stock that has gapped up, and that is then trying to fill in this gap. Whether the stock can fill this gap to the high o the previous day all or it can go to the close of the previous day, or it can only partially fill it up does not matter that much. The important thing with this strategy is that the market is trying to fill that gap, at least a little bit.

For this to work, you need to have the price go below your first ten-minute bar. On this method, it is not a good thing to see that first bar filling up the gap. A gradual attempt to fill up this gap after that first bar is better because it shows that the price is going in the right direction, but not too quickly.

When the stock starts to gap up and then works to close that gap, this means that you will be able to find a good amount of traders who are short and who feel that the stock will keep going down. When this stock turns around and moves into the range of your ten-minute bar, there are going to be some of these traders who left them in a position that is not the best. They may have already lost all of the gains that they earned, and they are trying to decide whether the stop they picked will end up making them money or not.

At this point, the breakout will come in. This breakout will be fast-paced, and it will occur at a higher than average volume. The traders that end up getting short squeezed will not be stopped out, and some of them will re-enter the market with a long position, which helps this breakout even more.

Gainer or gap up, afternoon breakout

This is another simple option that you can choose to go with. Just like with some of the other strategies, you will scan the gainer and the gap, except, you will do so in the late morning or early on in the afternoon. With this scan, you will look for some simple patterns, specifically the basing and consolidating type of patterns. You want to be able to find a strong rise in the price throughout the morning, and then the price needs to be able to settle to a less volatile period later on in the morning.

Often the stocks that have a really strong performance in the morning with a higher than average volume will often make a high that is a bit more than average before settling back slowly and just relaxing for a bit. They may look like they aren't going anywhere and this is the kind of stock that you are looking for. If you see that the stock is inching back up to the resistance, it is time to put in your buy stop order and wait around for the breakout that might come.

Of course, with this method, there is a few stocks that are not going to make it to the starting line. This is not a big deal because you can always switch out later and try it again with another stock. However, there will be some stocks that will explode up quickly and can help you to make a lot of money in a short amount of time.

If you have been working with trading or some time, then this is a strategy that you may have seen in the past, and you may not think that it will work that well for you. But you do not always need to have a complicated formula or strategy to make money with day trading. Sometimes the simple options, like this strategy, will be plenty to help you get some results.

Fibonacci retracement pattern

Here we will take a look at a thirty-minute chart. On this chart, you will want to look for some stocks that have reached a higher high than it has over the previous two days. You want to have a 15 sma cross above the 35 sma on that day. What you are looking for is the price to give you a retracement back to 38 to 62 percent on the following morning. You will recognize this part by looking at the 30-minute chart and seeing if there is an inverted U or an M pattern.

Once the price pulls back to this retracement level on the next morning, then you will want to look for the price to form a rising bar on your MACD histogram. Remember that the numbers do not need to be perfect. Sticking near the 38 and 62 percent is a good indicator, but if it goes a little below or above these numbers, you will be fine. The main point here is that you are waiting o see a good retracement with movement back towards where the impulse move came from. Once you can find this kind of setup on your chart, it is time to have a breakout trigger on your ten-minute chart.

At this time, you will want to switch over to your ten-minute chart. While looking at this, you will want to wait for a breakout of the high of your thirty-minute bar that was formed with this setup. You will then be able to enter the market and wait for the breakout to occur and for you to make a profit.

Gap down, fill gap, inside bar, breakout

To some people, it may seem like a bad idea to purchase a stock that is gapped down, but if these stocks have met some specific criteria, a short squeeze action can help to send up these stocks during the day and can help you to make a profit.

This option is easier than it seems. You will want to bring out your ten-minute charts. If you see that a stock has a gap down that fills in the gap and then the second or the third ten-minute bar forms as your inside bar, you know that you have a setup that you can work with. You will want to place your buy stop above the high of this particular inside bar. The trigger to make a purchase is when a breakout occurs above the high of that inside bar. You can place the stop order below that low of the inside bar, or you can choose another area to make your loses as low as possible.

Some other methods to use

But there are still so many other strategies that you will be able to use to see results. You will be able to use these in many cases based on what kind you feel the most comfortable with and what stocks are available in the market. Some of the other trading strategies that you can choose to go with include:

• News trading: this is where you will spend some time following the news to see what is going on with the market. Any time that there is a major news event, you will find that it can affect the stock market. Of course, you want to really look through the news; if the news is front page, you are already too late the price of the stock is already going up. However, as you get used to reading through the news and looking for the right hints, you will be able to see when a major trend is about to happen and then you can purchase or sell your stock based on what will benefit you the most.

• Range trading: this is a strategy that you can use a lot when you have the time and patience to do some in-depth research. With this one, you will follow a stock for some time and then figure out what the normal high and low range of that stock are during the day. You would then make sure that you do your trading within these limits.

• Pairs trading: as you can guess, this strategy will need you to work in pairs. You will choose a category that you want to trade in, and then you will go short on the stock that is considered weak and then long on the stock that is considered strong. When you make these trades at the same time, it is considered easier to make profits in the process.

• Contrarian trading: earlier we talked about a strategy where you were going to take the same actions of the market. If the market was going up, you were going to make a purchase, and if the market is going down, you will sell your stocks. With this strategy, you will trade against what the market is suggesting. So when the market is going up, you will sell your stock, and when the market is going down, you will make a profit. This one is hard for some day traders to go with because it does go against what they are used to with trading, but it can work if done properly.

• Chart patterns: another tool that can be really useful when you are day trading is the chart pattern. It is a good option when you want to be able to find your entry and exit points on the investment. If you use some technical indicators like the commodity-channel index, the relative-strength index, or the rate of change, you will be able to improve how reliable these chart patterns on. You can get a chart pattern from a variety of tools, even from your own platform, to help you figure out this information. You would only need to put the information on the chart to get some of the information that you need.

• Technical indicators: if you like to have a lot of information before you make your decisions with day trading, then technical indicators will be the best option for you. These technical indicators will be important to day traders because they can help show trends in the market that may be hard to see on their own. Looking at these indicators and making sure that you can interpret them the proper way will ensure that you can make a profit.

As you can see, there are a lot of different trading strategies. Many traders have worked over the years to create strategies that can help them to earn a profit with their stocks, and with all of the different types of stocks that are available, you are sure to find one that will work with the strategy that you would prefer. As a beginner, it is up to you to learn some more about these strategies and then pick out the one that you would like to use. With the right strategy and the right stock, you will be able to earn a good profit in no time with day trading.

CHAPTER 14: CREATING YOUR OWN DAY TRADING STRATEGY

As you start to get more into day trading, you may decide to develop your own strategy. There are a lot of great trading strategies that are out there, and we have discussed quite a few of them so far, but there may be some market conditions or other situations where you need to be able to develop your own strategy. Or, after trying out a few different things, you end up finding a new strategy, or a combination of strategies, that ends up working out the best.

Over time, it is important that you find your own place inside the market. As you go through, you may even find that you would rather be more like a swing trader rather than a day trader just because of the different methods that are available. The good news is, there is a market for any kind of trader, and there are a million types of strategies that you can use based on your own personal preferences along the way.

Before you jump into the market as a beginner with your own trading strategy, it is important that you start out by picking one of the strategies that are in this guidebook (or another proven strategy that you have researched). You need to have some time to try out a strategy and tread through the market a bit before you start coming up with your own strategy. Even if you have invested in the stock market before, you will find that working with day trading is completely different compared to some of the other methods available, and you do not want to pick a strategy that may have worked with one of your other trades, but will make you fail miserably with day trading.

It is all about spending some time in the market and getting familiar with the market. You will want to get familiar with how the day trading market works, how to recognize good stocks and so on before you make a good strategy that can help you. After spending some time in the market, working with one or two strategies that you like, you will be able to learn the patterns that you like and what to watch out for, and it becomes so much easier to make a strategy that will actually work.

But no matter where you are as a trader, it is so important that every trader has a strategy of some sort to help them get started. It is so easy for beginners to just pick out a stock and then start trading, without having a plan in place at all. This is a dangerous thing to work with. It pretty much leaves the decisions up to your emotions, and we all know how dangerous this can be when you are first starting out. You should never leave your trades up to the emotions; this will make you stay in the market too long or leave the market too early, and you will end up losing money.

In addition, you need to pick one strategy, whether it is one from this guidebook or one that you made up on your own, and then you need to stick with that strategy. Learn all of the rules that go with that strategy, how to make that strategy work for you, and exactly how you should behave at different times in the market with that strategy. Even if it ends up leading you to a bad trade (remember that any type of strategy and even the best traders will end up with a bad trade on occasion), you will stick it out until the trade is done. You can always switch strategies in between trades, but it is never a good idea to switch your strategy once you are already in the market.

Switching strategies can seem tempting when you are a beginner in the market. You may see that things are going south or may realize once you are in the market that you should have done a different strategy from the beginning. But as you look through some of the strategies that are in this guidebook, you probably notice that they are a bit different, and they need some different requirements before you can get in and out of the trade. Switching in the middle is not going to work and will lead to an automatic loss.

The most important thing that you can remember when you become a day trader is that all traders will fail at some point. Many beginners will fail because they do not take the time to learn how to properly day trade or they let their emotions get in the way of making smart decisions. But even advanced traders will have times when they will fail and lose money as well. The market is not always the most reliable thing in the world. Even when you are used to reading the charts and looking at the market, there will be times when it does not act as expected and a trader will lose out. Or the advanced trader may choose to try out a new strategy, and it does not work that well for them.

There will be times when you will lose money, and this can be hard to handle for a lot of beginners. This is also why you need to consider how much you can actually afford to lose on a trade before you enter the market. You do not want to go all out on your first trade because it is likely you will fail and lose that money or maybe more depending on the trade.

If you are worried about getting started in the market or you want to mess around and try out a few of the strategies ahead of time to see how they work, especially if you are using one of your own strategies, then you should consider working with a simulator. Sometimes you will be able to get one of these from your broker to try out and experiment with the market, and sometimes you may have to pay a bit from another site to use this simulator. However, this can be a valuable tool that will help you to try out different things, make changes, and get a little familiarity in the market before you invest your actual money. As a beginner, if you have access to one of these simulators, it is definitely worth your time to give it a try.

Picking your trade based on the time of day

Before we move on, we will take a look at which types of strategies seem to work the best at different times of the day. As you get into the market, you will notice that each time period of the day will be different and there are some patterns that seem to show up over time with them. We will work with three times of day, the open, the mid-day, and the close. If you want to be successful with day trading, it is not a good idea to use the same strategy at all three times of the day because these strategies will not be successful at all times of the day. The best traders will figure out what time of day they get the most profitable trades and then they will make some adjustments to their strategies and their trading to fit them into these profitable times.

First, let's talk about the open. This time period will last about an hour and a half, starting at 9:30 in the morning on New York Time. This is a busy time of the day because people are joining the market for the first time or they are making adjustments based on how their stocks had done overnight. Because this time is so busy, it can also be a really profitable time period if you play the game right. It is a good idea to increase the size of your trades during this time and do more of them because you are more likely to make some good money during this time. The best strategies to use during the open will be the VWAP trades and the Bull Flag Momentum.

Next session is the mid-day session, and this will start at 11 in the morning and go for about four hours. This is a slow time in the market, and it is considered one of the more dangerous times to trade during the day. There is not going to be much liquidity or volume in the market. Even a smaller order will make a stock move quite a bit during this time, so you really need to watch the market if you are holding onto your stocks.

It is more likely that you will be stopped with unexpected and strange moves during this period.

It is common for many traders, both beginners and those who are more advanced, to have a lot of trouble during the mid-day. Many decide that it is not the best idea to work in the market during this time. But if you do decide to trade, it is important to keep the stops tight and also to lower your share size. You should also be really picky about the risk and reward ratio during this time. You will find that new traders will often do their overtrading during this time, and it may be best to simply avoid trading during this time period altogether.

If you do decide to trade during the mid-day, it is best to watch the stocks as closely as possible, get some things ready for close, and always be very careful about any trading decisions that you try to do. You will find that support or resistance trades, moving average, VWAP, and reversal strategies work well during the mid-day.

And finally, there is the close, which starts at 3 in the afternoon and goes for about an hour. These stocks are considered more directional, so it is best to stick with those that are going either down or up during this last hour. It is possible to raise the tier size compared to what it was at in mid-day, but you do not want to go as high as you were at open. You will find that the prices at closing are often going to reflect what the traders on Wall Street think the value of the stocks is. These traders have stayed out of the market during the day, but they have been closely watching things so that they can get in and dominate what happens during the last little bit of trading.

It is also common to see that many market professionals will sell their stocks at this time and take the profits because they do not want to hold onto the trades overnight. As a day trader, you will be one of these professionals because you need to sell all of your stocks on the same day to be a day trader.

If you notice that the stock starts to move higher during this last hour, this means that the professionals are considered bullish on that stock. However, if you see that the stock starts to move lower in that last hour, it means that the professionals in the market are considered bearish. It is best during this last hour to work with trades that go with these professionals, rather than doing trades that go against them. When you decide to trade in the closing hour, you will want to use the moving average trades, support and resistance trades, or VWAP to get the best results.

As a beginner trader, you may find that you will profit during the open and then end up with a lot of losses during the rest of the day. You do not want to be one of them because this can wipe out all of the profits that you earned earlier. A good rule of thumb that you can stick with to keep things conservative with your losses is that you should never lose more than 30 percent of what you made in the open during the rest of the day. If you reach that 30 percent, you will stop trading for the day to protect your assets.

CHAPTER 15: COMPLETING THE SUCCESSFUL TRADE

Now that we have taken some time to look at the various parts of day trading and some of the good strategies that you can use, it is time to look at exactly how to get done with the trade. This chapter is going to show you all the steps, from start to finish, that you can utilize to get the most out of your trading. It will use some of the things that we had discussed earlier on in this guidebook and bring them all together to give the best results. So, let's take a look at the different steps that you need to take to complete a successful trade.

Build your watchlist

The first thing that you should do when you get up in the

morning is work on a watchlist. This will help you to limit some of the different options that you have available for day trading into just the ones that you are interested in using.

A good way to create this watchlist is to use your scanner. We talked about these a bit before, but having a good scanner can make a big difference when it comes to picking out the right stocks. You can put in some of the requirements that you are looking for when it comes to a stock, and it will alert you when one of these options become available.

Of course, you do not want to just pick out the stocks that show up on your scanner. These are a good place to start, but you need to actually take a look at these stocks and make sure that they will fit your needs. Some will be worth your time and others are not going to do that well. You need to be the one in control with your investment so while the scanner can give you a good start to your watchlist, you need to take the reigns and pick out what is the best.

Decide which stocks look the best

After you have had some time to make a watchlist and check all of our criteria for the stocks, it is time to decide which one looks the best. You may have a specific strategy that you want to go with, so you pick a stock that goes with that one the best, or you may have some other method.

One thing to remember with this is that you should not trade for at least the first five minutes of the opening and some people wait even a little bit longer than this. There is a lot of commotion that goes on in that first little bit of opening. New investors who are excited to get into the market will make their purchases then, and other traders may buy or sell based on how their stocks did overnight. It is really hard to predict where the market will go right at opening.

Once the opening session is done, you will be able to go through and pick out the stocks that you want to use. The commotion that goes on during the first bit of opening will help to determine how the rest of the day goes, but you just do not want to get caught up in it since things are kind of a mess during that time.

Set your enter and exit strategy

Before you go through and make a purchase, you need to make sure that you have all the strategies picked out. First, you need to have an enter strategy. This is the point where you will feel comfortable purchasing the stock. You want to keep this as low as possible because that helps to reduce your risk and can ensure profits more readily than a higher price. You should be looking at some of the charts that we discussed to see what a good price for the stock will be that day.

You also need to come up with an exit strategy. It is important to have a stop for losing money and one for earning money. First, let's look at the stop for losing money. There are times when the strategies that you pick or the decisions that you make are not going to turn out how you wanted, and the stock may start to lose money. The point of this stop is to ensure that you can control how much money you will lose in the process. Once the stock ends up reaching this number, you will withdraw from the market, no matter what the stock does later on.

Without this stop, you could end up with a little bit of trouble. Many new traders see that the stock is going down, and they keep riding it out. They hope that the market will turn around. Sometimes the market will turn around, but then there are times when the market will stay low or keep going down. And without a stop, you could be without a whole bunch of money. Depending on how far the market goes, you may not be able to cover the losses either. It is much better to have that stop in place and then exit the market at a comfortable loss rather than letting things get out of hand. You can always get back into the market later on if things begin to improve.

You also need to have a profit stop. This may seem a little bit silly because of course, you want to be able to earn as much profit as possible. But the day trading market is all over the place, and it is hard to predict. Yes, the market may go way above what you have as a profit stop, but it may go down just as quickly. This stop is there to protect you against those sudden falls that may take all of your profit. You may miss out on a bit of profit in the process, but it ensures that you are not going to lose out on everything.

Purchase your stocks

After taking some time to create a watchlist of stocks to go with and you have decided which one is best, it is time to make the purchase. Make sure that you use some of the criteria that we discussed earlier in this guidebook for picking out the right stock and determining how many of each stock you would like to purchase.

If you are working with a broker, you will simply need to submit an order to them to get started. This order will include information like which stocks you want to purchase, how many shares you would like to purchase, how much you want to spend on the stocks, and then your exit points for profit and to prevent loss. Your broker will be able to get this information into the system for you and take care of a lot o the work.

Some traders choose to do some of the work on their own, and that is fine too. Make sure that you have a good platform that will let you do all of this quickly. If the platform is slow or a mistake is made, it could really ruin your whole day in terms of how much you can make.

Watch the market

Day trading is much different than other types of stock trading. You may be used to hearing about long-term stock trading where you would put the money in and then leave it there for many years, maybe for retirement or something else. This can be successful for some people, but when it comes to day trading, you will be required to make decisions quickly and to buy and sell your stocks all on the same day. How do you expect to do this if you are not watching what the market does?

The market is pretty steady for the most part if you are looking at the long-term. Most stocks will see some little fluctuations and downturns, but for the most part, good stocks will keep on a steady pattern upwards. However, if you look at the daily trends of these stocks, you will see that there is a lot of up and down movement throughout the day. This is pretty normal for a stock and is how a day trader can make money so quickly.

It is your job as a day trader to watch these daily ups and downs. This will help you to determine which stocks to purchase in the first place and can help you to determine the best time to sell your stocks and make a good profit. When you are watching these stocks, you will better be able to determine when a downturn will occur and can get your money out of there before you lose everything. Once you put your money on the market, make sure that you are constantly watching the stock to see that it behaves in the way that you expect.

Sell the stocks at the predetermined points

Earlier you were supposed to set up your enter and your exit strategies. These are important numbers because they help you to reduce some of the risks that you are dealing with and will ensure that you are not going to lose more money than you are comfortable with. It is so important, regardless of what the market is doing at the time, that you follow these enter and exit points. If you ignore them, you will probably get a big loss on the books.

It is a good idea to listen to your exit point not only when the market is going down, but also when the market is going up. Some people understand why they should follow the exit strategy when the market is going down; they do not want to end up losing too much money in the market. But it is a bit harder on them when the market is going up. They may have placed a stop for how much profit they wanted to make, but then they see the market still goes up, and they do not want to get out at that time.

While it may be hard, make sure that you are listening to your exit strategy, even when the market is going up. Sure, the market may go past that point, but then it may hit a sharp downturn, and you could lose all of that profit. This is another method in place to ensure that your investment stays safe. If the market continues to do well and keeps going up, you will be able to jump back in later on.

Reflect on what you did right or wrong

After you are done with one trade, whether you earned a profit or you lost some money, it is a good idea to take a few minutes to think about how the transaction went. There are always things that you can learn along the way, and it is a good idea to reflect on these before you move on to your next trade. Plus, this will prevent you from jumping from one trade to another too quickly and making rash decisions.

One of the best things that you can do is write down this information. This may take a little bit longer, but the extra information you will have at your disposal will be so worth it. Over time, you will be able to write down a lot of information about your trading endeavors, and you can use that information later on if you get stuck about what to do on a particular trade. You are never going to be able to remember all of the trades that you will do with day trading and there is nothing better than real experience so take some time to reflect on the different things that you did on each trade (or at least after most trades) so that you can always have that information ready.

Start with another trade

If there is enough time during the day, such as you did a quick trade during the open of the day, then go ahead and go through these steps again. Day trading is all about doing a lot of quick trades all day long and since many of them can be done in just a few minutes, or maybe an hour or less, you have plenty of time to do more than one trade in the same day if you want. Just make sure that you are looking through the options, going through the steps above, and still taking the same precautions later on in the day as you did when you first got started.

One thing to note though is if you had a really bad stock in the morning, one that did not go your way, it might be a good idea to stay out of the market for the rest of the day and just do some practicing. This is especially true when you are first getting started as a beginner. Those losses can hit you hard, and you may find that your emotions will take over, without you even realizing it.

There are a lot of traders who end up in trouble because they got into a second trade too quickly. They may have been upset that they lost all that money, and now they are making decisions not based on facts and their research, but rather they are making decisions based on their emotions and the idea that they want to earn that money back. This leads you to make rash choices, and you will end up losing out on even more money in the process. If one of those big losses does occur, just take a break for the day and give yourself some time to think clearly. You can always get back in the market the next day.

Getting started in day trading can be an exciting time. It allows you to make a good investment and really get to know the market in a way that even other stock market investors do not. When you are ready to get started with day trading, and you want to actually make sure that your actions are profitable, make sure to follow the steps in this chapter and in the rest of the guidebook to help you get started.

CHAPTER 16: EASY DAY TRADING TIPS TO HELP YOU SUCCEED

When you are ready to get started with day trading, it is important that you are prepared. This is not an investment option that has a lot of room for mistakes along the way. You have to make your purchases and your sales all in one day, and that means a lot of quick thinking along the way. When you are ready to get started as a day trader, here are some tips and tricks that you can follow to be successful with as many trades as possible with day trading.

Pick the right stocks

Remember that while it is important to manage your risks and pick out a good strategy, you also need to make sure that you are picking out the right stocks. There are thousands of stocks available on the market for you to choose from, but not all of them will work for day trading. And just because you did well with one stock on one day does not mean it will be successful on the succeeding day or later on.

There are a few things that you can do to pick out the stock that will be the best for you. The first thing that you need to do is pick out the strategy that you would like to use; this will often help you to pick out a good stock. You can then use a scanner to help you find stocks that match your requirements. You should take a look at each stock before making the purchase, no matter how much it matches up with the scanner, so ensure that it will match the type of stock that you are looking for.

It does not matter how good of a strategy you pick or how much you work to manage your risk if you do not take the time to pick out a good stock, you will fail with day trading. Always do your research to make sure that you get the perfect stocks to increase your profits.

Stick with your strategy

As a day trader, there are a lot of great strategies that you can choose from to see success. We talked about quite a few of them in this guidebook, and you can even combine a few to help come up with your own strategy. As long as you learn which stocks to do with which strategies and you really learn how to make each of the strategies work properly, you will find that any of them has a good chance of success.

The biggest issue that comes with this is that you end up changing your strategy in the middle of a trade. Each strategy is different and combining them right in the middle of your trade will lead to trouble and will most likely make it so that you lose money along the way.

It is fine to switch strategies in between trades, but when you are in the middle of a trade, you need to stick with the trade that you originally picked. It does not matter if that trade is not working out the way that you would like or if you are losing money. Stick with that strategy until the trade is done and then learn from your mistakes if things do not go the way that you would like.

Keep the emotions out

One of the most important things that you can do when you get into day trading is to make sure that your emotions will stay out of the game. As soon as you let those emotions into the game, they will take over, and you are sure to lose out on any profits along the way.

When you allow your emotions to start coming into play, you are basically losing all of your control to make smart decisions. No one can make good decisions when the emotions are involved, and with all the stress and issues that can come with day trading, those emotions will hit some extremes pretty quickly. This is why it is so important to go through and pick out a winning strategy and to stick with it. This will keep the emotions at bay, and you can make the decisions ahead of time, before the emotions of being in the market come into play.

If you are in a trade and find that your emotions are starting to get in your way, it is time to make some changes. In some cases, you will be able to stick with your stop points and be safe for the rest of the trade. But if you have already gone through and left the stop points behind, it is time to leave the trade, no matter where it is going, and restart. You may even need to take a little time off from day trading, especially after a trade that did not do that well, so that you can regroup and get back to the critical thinking.

Come up with the right stop points

The stop points that you work with will make a big difference in how well your strategy will work. You need to have a stopping point for your profits and for your losses, and you need to decide these stop points before you even enter the market. This helps to keep the emotion out of the game and ensures that you will be able to make smart decisions rather than getting caught up in all of the heat of the moment.

The first stop point that you should consider is the loss stop point. This will be the low point of the exchange, the point where you will just cut your losses and walk out of the market. It does not matter where the market goes after this point, you need to get out of the market as soon as the stock reaches this point and just take the losses. When deciding on this point, you need to pick a point that is no lower than the lowest point for the stock in recent times. You also need to pick a low stop point that will only make you lose an amount that you are comfortable with, or you are adding in more risk than you need.

Another thing that you need to consider is the profit stop

point. This is the amount of money that you will take in profit before getting out of the market. It does not matter if the market keeps going up after you get out of the market. You will still need to make sure that you get out of the market and just take your profits. You can always join the market later on and try again, but making a decision on how much profit you will make before getting into the market will keep the emotions out of the game.

Consider working with a broker

If you have never worked in the market or looked at stocks before, it is probably a good idea to work with a broker. The process of day trading can be difficult to work with, and you have to make a lot of decisions quickly since you are doing the whole trade in one day. Your broker will be able to offer advice to you, help you to complete the trades that you want, and so much more.

Of course, you need to make sure that you pick out a good broker. There are a lot of different types of brokers and some of them will be amazing and will offer you advice that helps you to make money, and others will be cheap and ineffective. Do your research and look around and you are sure to find the results that you would like.

Take a break when needed

Losing out on some money can be really hard. Many beginners have some issues with this because they had high hopes of being able to make a lot of money in the process. They may even have spent hours doing research and learning the right strategy to be successful. And then something happened in the market, and things went south, causing them to lose money.

The first thing to remember is that everyone has a bad trade. There are people who have been in the day trading market for years who end up making bad trades. This is just a part of the business. The market does not always behave in the manner that you are hoping, no matter what, and there will be times when you run into a bad trade.

Depending on how the trade went, you may want to consider taking a break before entering again. It is hard to lose money, and if you jump back in too quickly, you could end up making some bad decisions, one that will result in you losing more money. There are no rules or how many times that you have to trade during the day to be a day trader. If you have a bad trade right in the morning and that was the only trade that you did, it is still fine to take a break and start up fresh the next day. It is better to miss out on a few hours of day trading rather than risk it because your emotions are in the way and lose more money in the process.

Write down tips after your trades

We mentioned this one a bit before, but it is always a good idea to write down information and tips when you are done with your trades. As a day trader, you will do a lot of trades. As you progress through this type of investment, you may do many trades all on the same day depending on how much money you have available and how much you would like to earn in the process. Through all of these trades, you are sure to learn a lot of things and even make a lot of mistakes.

Even as a more experienced day trader, there will be times when you have questions about what you should do. Rather than just guessing, why not take a look at some of the notes that you have taken in the past? Especially in the beginning, you should take some time to write down some notes about your trades. While you may not have time to write down the information after each trade, consider writing down a few notes at the end of the day. Writing about your mistakes and some of the things that you can do to make things better the next time will prove really helpful in the long run.

Day trading is a very lucrative investment, as long as you know what to expect and you can pick out the right options. By following these steps, you will be able to make the smart decisions that can make working in day trading very successful.

CONCLUSION

Thank you for making it through to the end of this book, let's hope it was informative and able to provide you with all of the tools you need to achieve your goals whatever they may be.

The next step is to get started with day trading. It can be a great investment opportunity, and this guidebook will provide you with all of the information and tips that you need to get started and see some success in day trading. Day trading is not something that you should just jump into; it is a stressful option that will require a lot of dedication, research and more to get the profits that you want.

This guidebook provides you with all of the information that you need to get started in day trading. It will start out with some of the basics of day trading and the personality traits that you need to be a successful day trader. You also will learn how to manage your risks and how to buy the best stocks before learning what tools and platforms are needed by expert traders to get the positive results.

After this guidebook went through some of the basics to help you make your decision about whether day trading was the best option for you or not, it will spend time talking about some of the best day trading strategies that will help you get amazing results. There are so many different strategies that are available for you to choose from. Any of them, from the reversal trading to resistance trading and more, can be successful as long as you learn the rules that go with them and stick with those rules, without making changes along the way.

Getting started with day trading can take some time, and it takes a lot of concentration. Make sure to read through this guidebook to learn some of the basics that you need to know about day trading and to help you pick out the strategies that you need to help you enter the market. With the tips and tricks in this guidebook, you will be ahead of the game to help you earn a great profit through day trading.

Finally, if you found this book useful in any way, a review on Amazon is always appreciated!

FOREX TRADING

A Beginner's Guide

© Copyright 2017 by Lee Digital Ltd Liability Company - All rights reserved.

The transmission, duplication or reproduction of any of the following work including specific information will be considered an illegal act irrespective of if it is done electronically or in print. This extends to creating a secondary or tertiary copy of the work or a recorded copy and is only allowed with express written consent from the Publisher. All additional right reserved.

The information in the following pages is broadly considered to be a truthful and accurate account of facts and as such any inattention, use or misuse of the information in question by the reader will render any resulting actions solely under their purview. There are no scenarios in which the publisher or the original author of this work can be in any fashion deemed liable for any hardship or damages that may befall them after undertaking information described herein.

Additionally, the information in the following pages is intended only for informational purposes and should thus be thought of as universal. As befitting its nature, it is presented without assurance regarding its prolonged validity or interim quality. Trademarks that are mentioned are done without written consent and can in no way be considered an endorsement from the trademark holder.

The author of this book has taken careful measures to share vital information about the subject. May its readers acquire the right knowledge, wisdom, inspiration, and succeed.

INTRODUCTION

Congratulations on downloading this book and thank you for doing so.

The following chapters will teach you the ins and outs of forex trading and how you can turn the forex market into a goldmine of profits:

Chapter 1 discusses the basics of forex trading. Learn about the forex market, how trading currencies work, ask vs. bid price, how to read forex pairs, and many others. This part of the book is will give you the knowledge that you need to become a forex trader.

Chapter 2 is about the advantages and disadvantages of forex trading. This chapter talks about the things that you should expect when you enter the forex market.

Chapter 3 lays down a set standard to look for when choosing a forex broker. Before you can start trading currencies, you first need to open an account with a legitimate and reliable broker.

Chapter 4 reveals effective strategies that you can use to turn the odds in your favor and increase your chances of making a profit.

Chapter 5 lays down the best practices that you should observe as trader. These practices can further increase your chances of success and effectively minimize your risks.

May this book be your guiding light to success and financial freedom.

There are plenty of books on this subject on the market, thanks for choosing this one! Every effort was made to ensure it is full of as much useful information as possible. Please enjoy!

CHAPTER 1: FOREX BASICS

What is Forex?

The term *forex,* or also known as *foreign exchange, currency trading,* or simply *FX,* refers to the activity of trading the world's currencies. Trading currencies is important for business and foreign trade. This is what keeps businesses, as well as the world's different currencies in existence. For example, if you are an American tourist and you visit Egypt, you cannot pay the stores in USD as it is not the local currency that is accepted in Egypt. Instead, what you need to do is to exchange your USD for the local currency in Egypt, which is the Egyptian pound at its current exchange rate. Here is another example: Let us say that you live in the US and you want to buy a certain commodity from India, you will need to pay the Indian merchant in Indian rupees. Also, in order for the merchant to acquire the said commodity, then he will also have to pay in Indian rupees if he is buying it within India. However, if the Indian merchant is also going to import the said commodity, then he will have to convert his currency into the acceptable local currency of the seller. This constant need to exchange one currency for another makes the FX market the largest and most liquid financial market in the world.

Forex is also an excellent way to make a profit. As the most liquid financial market, there is a high potential to make a positive profit by trading currencies. In fact, there are professional traders out there who make a living solely from this activity. So, just how much can you make by trading currencies? You can make a few dollars up to thousands and even millions of dollars every month. The amount you can profit depends on your invested capital, as well as the outcome of a trade. It is worth noting that forex is also a type of investment. Hence, just like any other kind of investment, there is also the possibility of losing all your money. The good news is that there are things that you can do and strategies that you can apply that can significantly increase your chances of making a profit. These will be discussed in more detail later in the book. For now, you should first have a good foundation and understanding of what forex is all about.

The Forex Market

The forex market is the place where currencies are traded. So, where is this forex market located? One thing that you should understand is that the forex market is a decentralized market. What this means is that there is no central marketplace where forex is conducted. It does not have a physical place or location. Instead, it is made electronically online across a network of computers around the world. Therefore, if you want to trade cryptocurrency, you only have to use the Internet in order to access the forex market. As for the schedule, you have to consider that the forex market has a worldwide scope and that different countries can have different timezones. The forex market is open round the clock starting from Sunday at 5pm EST up to Friday at 4pm EST. The forex market is a continuously moving market, so you can expect to see how the price quotes of the different currencies change at any time of the day or night.

The forex market has two levels: the interbank market and the over-the-counter market (OTC). The interbank market is where banks trade. The OTC market is where regular traders engage in the FX activity. This is where you will trade using an online platform. Before you can trade currencies online, you will have to make an account with an FX broker. It is your broker who will provide you with the platform that you can use for trading.

Among the different types of currencies, the US dollar is the most traded currency. It comprises more than 80% of all trades. It is followed by the Euro, and then by the Japanese Yen.

The forex market is the most active market in the whole world, which makes it a highly profitable place for professional traders. However, you should keep in mind that it is also a challenging place. It is not a secret that there are a number of investors who have lost a big amount of their invested capital in just a few days; worse, some of them have lost all their invested money. Still, for those who understand what they are doing and give it enough focus, effort, and practice, the forex market is the perfect place where you can continuously rake in serious profits.

Is it for you? Although you are welcome to join and participate in the forex market, it does not always mean that it is also the place that will make you earn money. When you trade foreign currencies, there is only one of two possible outcomes: either you make money or lose it. The unfortunate truth is that not everyone can have success in the forex market. If you are the type who just wants to gamble and rely on luck, if you do not want to take time and efforts to study the market, then you will most likely lose your money in just a few days. However, if you are willing to exert serious efforts, if you can sit for hours and study what is going on in the forex market and make analysis, then you can significantly increase your chances of making a profit. Also, if you get really good at it, then you might even be able to turn the forex market into a path that leads financial freedom.

Forex Pairs

When you trade in the stock market, you need to understand forex pairs. They are composed of currencies that are being traded. The major currency pairs are the most liquid in the market, and they are the following: EUR/USD, GBP/USD, USD/JPY, USD/CHF, USD/CAD, and AUD/USD.

There are also currencies that are not traded with the US dollar, and so their pairs are considered as minor currency pairs. Although they are also considered as liquid, they are notas liquid as the major currency pairs. The minor currencies include the GBP/JPY, EUR/GBP, and EUR/CHF.

As a forex trader, you need to understand how to read forex pairs. Take note that a forex pair involves two different currencies, for example: EUR/USD. Every currency pair is composed of a *base currency* and a *quote currency*. The base currency, also known as the *bid price*, refers to the first currency in a pair; and the second currency, also known as the *ask* price, is the second currency in a pair. Therefore, in our example (EUR/USD), the base currency is the EUR while the quote currency is the USD.

When you trade currencies, you will see a number after pair. For example, you may see something like this: EUR/USD 1.25.

Take note that the base currency, which in this case is the EUR, is always equals to 1. Hence, you can view it as EUR 1/USD 1.25. What this simply means is that 1 EUR is equivalent to 1.25 USD.

What if you want to use USD as the base currency? In forex convention, it will then look like this, USD/EUR 0.80. Be careful not to just switch the two currencies and their values. Instead, you have to divide the base currency by the quote currency. Although they may seem different, their mathematical relation remains the same. If you divide 1 by 0.80, you will get back to the value of 1.25.

Ask and Bid

Now that you have a better understanding of a forex currency pair, it is time to understand the two important things about a forex quote: The ask and bid price. Let us use an example:

EUR/USD = 1.3400/07

In a normal situation, the difference between the ask and bid price is just a very small amount, usually less than 1/100th of a unit, it has become a normal part of a forex convention to just show the last two digits. In this case, it is 07. If you write this down in its complete form, it will look like this: EUR/USD = 1.34000/1.3407.

Here is something that you need to realize: The bid price does not refer to the price that you need to bid in order to purchase a currency pair. The bid and ask price should be taken from the perspective of your forex broker. Therefore, in order to make a profit from a transaction, a broker will *ask* higher than the price that he would be willing to *bid* if you were the one selling the currency pair. In our example, since you want to buy the EUR which refers to the base currency, then you will have to pay the *ask* price of the broker which is 1.3407 USD. If you are the one who is selling, then you need to accept your broker's bid of 1.3400. AS you can see, either way, it is in favor of your broker. Now, the difference between the ask price and the bid price is what is referred to as the *spread*. Obviously, it is the commission that your broker receives from a trade.

Forex: Buy and selling

What does it mean to buy and sell currencies in the forex market? Forex is about trading currencies, and it is participated by banks and individuals worldwide. When a trade is made in the forex market, there are always two sides to it: there is someone who buys a currency in a pair, and there is another who sells the other currency in a pair. As an FX trader, you make a profit by predicting whether the value of a currency in a pair will increase or decrease against the value of another currency. For example, let us say that you buy US$5,000 by selling $4,000 euros. In this example, the position that you have is that you predict that the value of the US dollar will appreciate (increase) against the euro. If your prediction is correct, then you will make a profit. Now, in order to realize your profit, you still need to sell your US dollars. In this case, you should sell your US$5,000 into euro. In exchange, you will then receive more than $4,000 euros. Needless to say, the value of US dollar must first increase against the euro before you sell them. As you can see, buying and selling foreign currencies is simple and easy to do. You just have to predict if the value of a currency will increase or decrease against the value of the other currency in a pair.

Percentage in Point

Percentage in point, simply referred to as simply *pip*. This refers to the measure of a *spread*. Take note that the spread refers to the difference between the bid price and the ask price and is the commission that your broker receives. The pip is the change in value the value of a particular currency. You might have heard some traders who say that they want to profit by 500 pips. So, what does a pip exactly mean? To illustrate, let us say that the price of a currency pair changes from 1.6000 to 1.6001, then that is a change by 1 pip. Hence, a pip is a unit of value that is used to show the change in the value of a currency pair. It is important to understand the pip because it signifies how much you can profit or lose. For example, if a trader buys the currency pair EUR/USD, he will profit if the price of EUR increases relative to the USD. To illustrate: Let us say that you buy in the pair EUR/USD, you buy the EUR for $1.7500. If you exit the trade at $1.7600, then that is a profit by 100 pips. Of course, if the value decreases, then the value of the pips would be on the negative, say -100 pips, and that signifies a loss.

So, how many pips should you aim for? There is no hard and fast rule as to the number of pips that you should gain. Of course, the longer you hold on to a currency pair the more significant the pip value may change since the price of the different currencies fluctuates slowly. Of course, there is also the possibility that their prices will go back to their original price, depending on their price movement. For small trades, many are already contented with 50 pips or even 30 pips. The key is to be on a positive profit.

Types of Orders

There are different orders that you can give to your broker as to how you want to trade currencies. These orders may be used to control how you enter and exit the FX market. Hence, they play an important element in building a successful career as a foreign currency trader.

- Market order

A market order is the most common type of order in forex. This order tells the broker to buy or sell a currency pair at the best possible price. This happens instantly and is always executed by the broker. A market order is the best way to enter the market as quickly as possible.

- Entry order

As the name implies, an entry order is a way to enter the market. It is difficult to spend the whole day monitoring the market just to see when you will enter it. In this case, you can just use an entry order and be able to spend your time away from the computer. In an entry order, you get to enter the market once the price reaches a certain point.

- Limit order

A limit order is often used to exit a market at a profit. This order directs your broker to buy or sell a specific number of units of a currency pair at a defined value. If you have a long position, then the limit order should be higher than the current market price. If you are taking a short position, then the limit order would be lower than the market price. This of it as a limiting line where you trade will be automatically closed once it reaches that line. Of course, once this line is reached, then you will receive whatever profit you may have into your account balance.

- Stop order

A stop order is used to exit a trade. It is also referred to as *stop-loss order*. The purpose of this order is to control or limit the possible losses that you may experience. Hence, it closes a trade that reaches a certain level of loss. Although a stop order is not a good sign when its defined limit is reached, it is able to limit your losses and closes a trade in order to prevent you from losing more.

Risk/Reward Ratio

The risk/reward ratio simply refers to the calculation of how much you should risk in a trade as compared to how much you should profit from it. For example, if you are making a trade and you set a stop loss at 15 pips and then set your take-in profit at 25 pips, then your risk reward ratio will be 15:25. This means that you are risking 15 pips in order to earn 25 pips.

When used in Forex, the key is to look for an opportunity where you reward will be much higher than the risk. It will be great if you always find trades where the reward always outweighs the risk but such is not always the case. Although it is commonly advised that a high reward and low risk trade is the most ideal, the contrary may be practical when you notice that the market is highly volatile. There is no strict rule as to the most ideal risk reward ratio should be. It may depend on the type of trader that you are, as well as the trading strategy that you use. Of course, as a professional trader, it is still ideal to make more trades where the reward is much higher than the risk in order to increase your chances of ending up with a positive profit after you sum up all your winnings and losses.

Leverage

One of the reasons why many people like to engage in forex is because it gives them a higher leverage unlike other financial instruments. But what does the term *leverage* mean? A leverage allows you to borrow money that you can invest from your broker. Since you will be able to borrow money, you will be able to invest a higher amount, which means that you will have a higher potential profit since you will be earning a certain percentage of your investment. Forex is known for offering a high leverage, which means that for an initial margin, you can be trading a big amount of money. The leverage can vary from 50:1, 100:1, or even 200:1, depending on your broker and the size of your position. Take note that before you can start engaging in forex, you should first open an account with your broker; in this case, you need a margin account. So, what do these leverages mean? A 50:1 leverage signifies that the minimum margin requirement is only 2% (1/50) of the total value of trade in his trading account available as cash. Accordingly, a 1:100 leverage would only require 1%, and so on. The usual leverages used as 1:50 and 1:100. A leverage of 1:200 is used normally for positions that are around $50,000 or less.

In application, what this means is that if you want to trade $100,000 with a 1% margin (100:1 leverage), then you only need to invest $1,000 in your margin account. Obviously, this leverage is so much higher than the 2:1 leverage that you get when you put your money in equities or the 15:1 leverage when you invest in futures market. Now, although a leverage of 100:1 may seem very high and risky, do not forget that foreign currencies do not fluctuate so high in one trading day. Normally, they only fluctuate by less than 1% in a trading day.

An obvious advantage of leveraging is that it allows you to have a decent trading size even if you only have a substantial investment capital to begin with. Many professional traders recommend at a minimum of $1,000 as an initial capital for forex. However, the problem is that not all traders can afford to risk a thousand dollars. Also, risking $1,000 when you are just a beginner might not be the best choice to make. This is where leveraging comes into play.

But, can you still trade foreign currencies without leveraging? The answer, of course, is in the affirmative. There are some notable traders who do not leverage their position. Here is an example of how *not* leveraging can be an advantage: Let us say that you purchase 1,000 USD using 800 EUR without any leverage. Let us assume that the price of USD experiences a 50% drop in price, then you will only lose only 50% or just 400 EUR. This means that you are still in the game. Now, consider the same example but let us assume that you are using 100:1 leverage' even if the price changes by less than 1%, then you will lose all your funds. Of course, an obvious disadvantage of not leveraging is that you will earn a much lower amount than you would normally have. After all, if you cannot expect to profit a very high percentage of your invested funds. Normally, a professional investor only makes a decent and reasonable percentage profit. Hence, the bigger your fund is, the more money you can make.

What is a Lot?

A *lot* refers to the smallest size that you can trade in the forex market. Hence, it also has to do with your risk exposure. As a trader, you should find the best lot size that is suitable for you based on your current trading account. The lot size can also have an impact how much you will be affected by the forex market movement. For example, if you only have a small trade, a 100-pip movement would not be too significant. However, if you are holding a huge lot, a 100-pip movement can have a strong impact. In your career as a trader, you will surely encounter different lot sizes. As already stated, it is important that you understand them so that you will know which lot size is suitable for you:

- Micro lot

As the name already implies, this is usually the smallest lot that is offered by most brokers. A micro lot refers to a lot of 1,000 units of a currency that your account is funded with. Hence, if you are using US dollars, then a micro lot is equivalent to $1,000 USD. If you want to trade a pair that is dollar-based, then 1 pip is equivalent to 10 cents. If you are a beginner, then it is advised that you stick to micro lots.

- Mini lots

A mini lot is equal to 10,000 units of the currency in your

account. Hence, if you are trading an account that is dollar based, and if you are trading a pair that is also dollar-based, then a single pip in a trade will be equal to $1. Compare this with a micro lot where 1 pip is only 10 cents. It should also be noted that in forex trading, the market can move by more than a hundred pips per day. So, just imagine how much profit or losses you can experience. Obviously, trading mini lots requires a higher capital than trading micro lots.

- Standard lots

A standard lot is 100,000 units of the currency of your funding account. If you are trading in US dollars, that is equal to $100,000 USD. Hence, the average pip size for a standard lot is equal to $10 a pip. Therefore, when it says that you are up by 10 pips, then that is equivalent to $100 profit. However, in the case of losing 10 pips, then that would translate to $100 loss. To make trades using standard lots, you should have at least $25,000 as standard lots are mostly for large accounts. Most traders only trade using micro lots and sometimes mini lots.

Day Trading vs. Long-Term trading?

Just how long should you keep a position open and hold a

trade? You are probably familiar of the term *day trading*. It is where traders hold their positions only for one trading day. At the end of a trading day, they close out all their positions, regardless whether they are in a profitable position or at a loss. Of course, you are not compelled to keep a position just for one trading day; there are also traders who maintain a position for days, weeks, months, and even longer. Remember that there are certain advantages and disadvantages associated with day trading and long-term trading. Whether you should use day trading or long-term trading would depend mainly on the type of FX trader whom you are and the strategy that you use.

Day trading is also known as short-term trading. It involves being in a fast-paced environment as you open and close all positions within one trading day. One of the main reasons why traders enjoy day trading is its potential to generate profits quickly. If you want to have quick money, then day trading is probably the one for you. Another advantage is that you get to control your risk as you will only be risking something while you are in front of your computer, and you can easily monitor what is going on in your trades. The moment that you close out all positions and leave your computer, there would be nothing for you to worry about. Another reason why traders like day trading is that they get to have a fresh start every day. They are not affected by what has happened the previous day and consider each day as a fresh start and a new day to hit the market and rake in serious profits. Last but not least, day trading can prevent you from holding on to a continuously losing investment since you will be closing out all positions at the end of the trading day.

Now, let us look at the notable disadvantages of day trading. Day trading involves dealing with a fast-paced and high-stress environment. It is not uncommon to find new traders who dive in to short-term trading and see their funds being exhausted every day. Day trading takes knowledge, skill, and practice. Day trading compels you to make quick yet intelligent decisions. For a beginner, this may be difficult to do, especially if you intend to open multiple positions every day. The volatility of the forex market can also affect short-term trading. For example, you may be able to start in the right direction but due to the nature of day trading you might be closing out your position at a loss. In a trade, proper timing is essential as to when you enter as well as when you exit a trade. Although this may be easy to do when you are investing for a long term, this is a crucial part when you engage in day trading as it can be a deciding factor whether or not you will profit from a trade.

Long-term forex trading takes the nature of the basic buy and hold strategy. Here, you will not have to deal with a stressful environment. You can make as much time as you want to identify the best currency pair to invest in. Exiting the trade is also easy as you can wait as much as you want until you are satisfied with your profit. You can also care less about the day-to-day volatility that the forex market experiences and simply focus on your long-term vision. After all, it is very hard to predict to which direction the market is heading in just a short time as the effect of price-changing factors can have some delay. Long-term traders are also not required to make multiple trades every day. In fact, it is not uncommon to find long-term FX traders to only make less than 5 trades in a year. Unlike day traders who observe and analyze the market on a day-to-day basis, long-term traders are free to skip some days and not mind the market at all. Needless to say, being a long-term trader is much less stressful than a day trader. Long-term traders also have more time for themselves to do other things. They are not expected to be on the computer whenever the market is open. They can make a trade and come back to it whenever they want. Another notable advantage is that long-term traders usually enjoy the most profit per trade. Since the price of currencies fluctuates only slightly, it takes time to make a significant amount of profit. Last but not least, long-term trading has more chances to be able to recover from what otherwise would have been a bad trade. Take note that the price of currencies fluctuate continuously. Hence, just because it appears that a certain trade is at a loss, it does not mean that it will continue to be a losing trade. There is still a chance that it may recover and have you end up with a positive profit. For example, your worst trade today might just turn out to be the best trade after a few weeks.

Although it may seem that long-term trading is the better option, it cannot really be concluded that it is superior to day trading. After all, long-term trading also has its disadvantages. Long-term trading can easily get boring. If you are an active trader, the lack of action in long-term trading is not something that you will enjoy. You simply cannot wait for weeks and months just to know the outcome of a trade. Long-term trading is also vulnerable to so many elements including those that are unforeseen since so many things can happen over the course of a long-term trade. Hence, it is almost impossible to tell if your investment is really good enough or not as it may only be considered a good trade for a week but a bad investment the following week.

So, which one is for you? Again, the answer will primarily depend on the type of trader you are and the strategy that you are using. The situation and attending circumstances of each case can also be a determining factor as to which approach would be more suitable. It is noteworthy that you are not limited to using only a single approach. There are professional traders who open positions that will last only for a day, as well as positions that they tend to keep for a much longer term. It is up to you to make the decision. Instead of bothering whether you should use day trading or long-term trading, you might want to focus more on the attending circumstances. Many times the best approach to take when trading foreign currencies for a profit is to consider the current state of the FX market. From there, you will be more able to predict its direction and come up with the best trading decision.

There are other advantages and disadvantages that can be associated with day trading and long-term trading. This is only to give you an idea of what to expect when you trade for a day or for a longer term.

Going *Long* vs. Going *Short*

When you engage in FX trading, you will definitely hear or read about people "going long" or "going short." So, what does it mean to go long/short on a trade? When you go *long*, you buy the first currency while you sell short the second currency. This means that you buy it with a view that its price will soon increase. Now, in a *short* position, you sell the first currency and buy the second currency. Hence, when you go short it means that you predict that the price is going to decrease. Whether you should go long or short depends on the situation. If you think that the price is going up, then go long; however if you think that the price is going down, then go short. Simply put, going long means buying the first base currency in a pair as you think that it will be more valuable, while going short is selling as you think that it will be less valuable relative to the second currency in a pair.

Going long simply means buying a currency pair. Here is an example: Let us say that you see this currency pair: USD/JPY 90. Obviously, the base currency is the USD which is equal to 1 and the quote currency is the JPY which is equal to 90. This currency pair simply means that 1 USD is equivalent to 90 JPY (Japanese Yen). In this example, going long simply means that you believe that the USD $1 will soon be more valuable than the 90 JPY, which means that the value of JPY in the given currency pair will decrease as the value of USD increases, like this: From USD:JPY 90 into USD:JPY 95. As you can see, JPY will need more units just to match up with 1 USD. This means that for this particular pair, the value of USD has increased while the value of JPY has decreased.

Now, if going long is making a buy order, going short simply means making a sell order on a currency pair. This is just the opposite of going long. Let us use our previous example: USD: JPY 90. Now, if you think that USD will soon be less valuable than JPY, then you should short on the USD and go long on JPY. For example, if you think that USD: JPY 90 will soon be USD: JPY 85; this shows that value of USD has decreased related to JPY. So, you short on USD and go long on JPY.

Whether you should go long or short depends on the circumstances of each case. If buying and investing in the base currency appears to be a profitable option, then you should take a long position. However, if you think that the price is going to fall, then sell short. AS you can see, you need to understand the market. To do this, you should engage in research and analyze the data that you have.

Trading Psychology

Let us move to another important matter known as *trading psychology*. How does a mind of a trader work and what kind of a trader are you? Whether you make a profit or not does not depend solely on the situation of the forex market. After all, if only you can identify the currency that will increase in value, then you will be in a profitable position. When the price of a certain currency increases, then another currency will definitely decrease, and vice versa.

- Stay objective

Being a forex trader can sometimes be quite lonely. It is the kind of career where no one cares about you. The entire forex market would not care whether or not you make money or lose all of your investment. You need to stay objective and not allow your emotions to get in the way. Although it is good to have passion in what you do, it does not mean that you can allow your emotions to cloud your judgment. Being objective means sticking to your strategy. You should view the forex market as it actually is and not the way you want it to be.

- Quality over quantity

Many traders, especially those engaged in day trading, forget the importance of quality over quantity of trades. Keep in mind that you are not obligated to enter into a trade. Just because you have spent an hour or two trying to read the charts does not mean that you should make a trade. A common mistake committed by many FX traders is to make a transaction even if they do not feel confident that it will turn out positively in their favor. This is true especially if you are already so used to trading. Always remember to focus on quality over quantity.

- Greed

Greed is perhaps the number one enemy of a trader. Although the drive to make money is important, you should not allow it to interfere with your trading practices and strategies. Greed should not dictate how you handle your trades. It is not a secret that many traders and gamblers have lost all their profits and all their funds because of greed. In order to prevent yourself from being greedy, you need to exercise a good level of self-discipline.

- Panic

Panic is something that prevents traders from making sound decisions. It is also very common in the market. It usually happens when a significant event that has a negative impact upon certain currencies takes place. In such instance, many traders pull out their positions right away, which can further aggravate the effects of said event upon the FX market. As a professional trader, you should no longer panic even when it seems that the market is going down. Such things are part of the FX business. Although they are often unforeseeable, they are nevertheless expected to happen — you just do not know the exact manner by which they will occur. The problem with panicking is that it tends to make you make all the wrong decisions. The reason is that you will not be able to think clearly and view the market properly when you are in panic. Therefore, in order to avoid this, you need to learn to calm down, especially during stressful situations. Just because everyone else is panicking does not mean that you should respond in the same manner.

- Fear

Fear is like the opposite of greed. The problem with fear is that it prevents you from raking in more profits. When you trade currencies, the objective is to make a profit. However, although recognizing fear can be good, allowing it to prevent you from entering profitable trades would not serve your interest. Never let fear tell you to back out from a good trade. The truth is that there is no position that will guarantee a 100% return of positive profits. However, there are ways to increase your chances of picking profitable positions. In order to combat the effects of fear, you need to train yourself to understand that a successful career in trading is not something that just comes by luck or at random. It is a product of research, hard work, perseverance, skill, and lots of practice. Therefore, if you are truly committed to trading and enter positions with knowledge, backed up with more research and analysis, then you can face fear and tell it that it is wrong. Of course, sometimes, you also need to listen to fear in order to avoid getting too greedy. You should strike a balance between fear and greed.

- Overconfidence

Overconfidence usually take place after you enter several trades that turn out to be highly profitable. You would feel as if you already know everything that has to be known about the FX market. You may even feel unstoppable as if you were the master of the market. Although having confidence is good, being overconfident can make you lose all your money. It is also noteworthy that most of the time, overconfidence leads to greed. When you are overconfident, you get to become slack and fail to do enough research and analysis. It will tend to get you make careless decisions — and these decisions can mean losing a big part of your funds or even all of your funds. Therefore, be mindful of how confident you are. If you notice that you are already being overconfident, then the best thing to do would be to stop for a while and relax. You need to be calm and prevent yourself from entering trades with a poor preparation.

- Self-control

Successful and professional traders are masters of themselves. It is not uncommon to see a professional trader to just keep silent or even laugh after losing a trade. This is because he understands that in the course of one's trading career, you will definitely encounter losses along the way. The important thing is to end up with a positive profit once you add up everything. Encountering some losses is a natural part of the game. A professional FX trader is able to exercise control over himself and maintain his composure because he has knowledge, understanding, practice, and a rich experience of what FX trading is really all about.

- Bias

Many traders tend to be biased. Just because they want to trade a particular currency pair, they end up making all the reasons to justify their position. However, they fail to see the consequences of such trading decision. Professional traders are not attached to any currency. They only trade when there is a good opportunity to profit. More importantly, before entering into a trade, they consider all the elements that may affect the trade. They are also open to different views, even those that may contradict their own opinions.

- Develop your own understanding

When you are a beginner, the tendency is to rely on books and expert advice that you may find online from some FX trading "experts." However, professional traders know that the right psychology is to have your own understanding of the FX market. It should also be noted that considering today's world, it is very easy to promote one's self as an expert by simply harnessing the power and reach of social media. All you need is to launch an effective marketing strategy and you can be tagged as an expert. Unfortunately, being an expert is not just about being a popular figure when people talk about the FX market. Having many people visiting your forex blog does not make you an expert. The sad truth is that many of the "experts" out there are not real experts. In fact, they may even have more losses than profits. Of course, there are still real experts out there who make a living simply by trading currencies. However, they are not as many as you might think. Instead of relying on expert advice, the better approach is to develop your own understanding of the market. After all, even the real expert themselves also have contradicting views. Hence, instead of depending on experts, just take their pieces of advice as they are — just a mere advice. You can compare your own view with their advice and learn something from it. The important thing is to develop our own view and understanding of forex. This is an important key to becoming an expert.

CHAPTER 2: ADVANTAGES AND DISADVANTAGES OF FOREX TRADING

Forex trading has its advantages and disadvantages. It is important that you know about them, so that you will know what to expect once you start trading foreign currencies. Let us examine them one by one:

Advantages

- High-profit potential

Forex trading has a high-profit potential. In fact, there are professional FX traders who have quit their day job and trade currencies for a living. Some people have also attained financial freedom by forex trading. Trading currencies has long been established as something that can be very lucrative. Of course, you also need to spend time and efforts in order to make it worthwhile and profitable. When you engage in FX trading, even a small investment of $100 can grow by more than 300% in just a short period of time. Compare this with investing in stocks where a profit of 20% in a year is already considered high. Indeed, if you have money that you can use to invest, learning forex trading is most probably the best thing that you can do that can lead you to financial freedom.

- Leverage

It is not a secret that many people like forex trading because it will allow you to leverage. As we have discussed in the previous chapter, leveraging will allow you to invest a small amount of money but trade using a substantial capital. Needless to say, this will allow you to rake in more profits. Many traders do not have enough money to start up with a decent capital. Leveraging will allow you to spend and risk less and at the same time have a high-profit return.

- Low cost

The main cost in forex trading is normally included already in the spread. Therefore, you no longer need to worry about any exchange or clearing fee, and not even a brokerage fee. Under normal market conditions, the retail transaction cost is even lower than 0.1%. If you are working with a large dealer, then it is normally lower than 0.7%. Of course, this may increase depending on your leverage. Since you no longer have to worry about so many costs that you need to cover, you can put all your focus on what really matters, and that is making a profit.

- High liquidity

The FX market is famous for having high liquidity. Therefore, you can expect to be able to buy and sell currencies easily since there is always someone who will take the other side of your trade. You can never get "stuck" and there is definitely no waiting time for buying and selling currencies. It is a very active market.

- 24-hour market

The forex market is open round-the-clock. Hence, you can trade in the morning, in the afternoon, in the evening, or evening at 2am or 3am. It is up to you to decide when you want to participate in the market. Although the forex market follows a schedule, once it opens for the week, you can rest assured that it will remain open round the clock until it closes by the end of the week.

- Fair market

There is no authority that controls or unduly influences the forex market. Of course, certain things and event may affect the price of currencies, but they cannot continuously do so for an extended period of time. The forex market is very big with lots of different participants.

- Easy to enter

It is easy to enter the forex market. You can start participating in the market simply by going online. You can make trades in the comfort of your home. You also do not need a high capital. There are many online brokers that will allow you to trade even with a small investment.

- Convenient

Forex trading is convenient to do. All you need is to connect to the Internet and you can start trading using the trading platform that is provided by your broker. You can easily open and close positions with just a few clicks of a mouse.

- More choices

With around 28 major currency pairs to choose from, you will never run out of currency pairs to trade. This ensures that you will not find a moment to sit idly. Also, considering the nature of forex, you are sure that there is always a currency pair among the chances that will make profits.

- Demo account

Most forex traders will allow you to preview their services by providing you with a demo account. A demo account will allow you not only to test your broker's trading platform, but it will also allow you to trade in a real-market environment. A demo account can also be used to test your strategy. As a forex broker, testing your strategy before using it with real money is an important habit that you definitely have to do.

- Fun

Trading currencies is fun to do. In fact, it is very easy to get addicted to it. It is like a game that adults can truly enjoy, especially if you are making positive profits. It is fun to look at charts and choose the currency pair that you want to invest in. Developing a strategy and making your own market predictions can be fun. Overall, the whole activity of being a forex trader can be a truly fun experience.

Disadvantages

- Risky

Although people who engage in forex trading are in it for the profit that they can make, the unfortunate truth is that many of these traders end up losing their investment. It is risky to participate in forex, especially if you do not know what you are doing. In fact, if you do not have knowledge of forex and simply jump in without preparation, it is most likely that you will suffer a big loss in just a few days. If you get too careless, then you can expect to lose your money on the very first day of trading. Even those who have been trading for years are still careful before they open a position. As a beginner, you need to be more cautious of your actions.

Although you are well encouraged to do all the necessary research and analysis before making any trade, there is no amount of preparation that can guarantee 100% it will give you a favorable outcome. Literally every trade that you make has its risks.

- Lower return

It is true that you can make lots of money with forex even if you just invest a small amount since you can use the power leverage. It is also true that trading currencies has a higher profit potential than just investing in stocks. However, forex trading is not the one that offers the highest payout. Of you want a higher return, then you might want to consider options trading instead of forex trading. With options trading, you can get as high as 90% return for every trade that lasts as fast as two minutes, or even less. However, it is worth noting that options trading is so much riskier than forex trading. Options trading is like gambling in the casino. There is also no way to leverage your position.

- Volatility

The prices of different currencies are affected by many factors. The forex market can, from time to time, be highly volatile. You can also expect for some unforeseeable events to take place. The bad part is that traders may not be able to do anything about them when they occur. For example, during the time when Iceland got bankrupt, forex traders holding Icelandic krona could not do anything but watch how they were holding a something that has significantly depreciated. This is unlike in investing in stocks where shareholders can somehow pressure the board of directors to act more promptly and take appropriate actions. To avoid being a victim of the high volatility of the market, it is well advised that you limit your losses and always be sure to use a well-planned approach when trading.

- Less regulated

Since forex trading is not regulated by any central authority, traders usually rely on their broker to facilitate a trade. If you get lucky and end up working with an unreliable broker, you will only get scammed and cheated in the process. Also, since you will be relying on the assistance extended to you by a broker, you may not have total control over your trades and orders. Therefore, in order to prevent this from happening, it is important that you only work with regulated and legitimate brokers. Since forex takes place in an over-the-counter market, you need to be careful in choosing your broker.

- Self-taught

Unlike investing in stocks where you can ask for assistance from trade advisors and portfolio managers, dealing with forex is ultimately something that you do on your own. It is not a surprise for beginners to lose their initial investment. Unfortunately, after experiencing a bad loss, they usually get discouraged, which prevents them from fully learning the ins and outs of trading. Hence, when you are just starting out, it is important that you admit to yourself that you are just a newbie. As much as possible, take advantage of the demo account that is provided to you by your broker, so that you can familiarize yourself with the actual trading environment. It is also advised that you start out small even if you have a big amount of money that ready for trading in your account.

- Hard to predict

There are multiple factors that affect the forex market. In fact, this is the reason why forex traders usually rely on technical analysis. With so many factors that influence the prices of the different currencies, it becomes almost impossible to predict the price movement of a currency. Of course, you can always apply an effective strategy, but it does not change the fact that the forex market is hard, if not impossible, to predict.

If you were to consider all the elements that can influence the outcome of a particular trade, then you will have to spend lots of hours just to be able to analyze everything. However, the forex market is a continuously moving market. Therefore, by the time that you finish analyzing a set of data, there will definitely be a new set of information that you could look into.

CHAPTER 3: FOREX TRADING BROKER

What to Look for in a Forex Trading Broker

Learning to choose your forex trader broker is a very important part of forex trading. Before you can even start to trade currencies, you first need to open an account with a forex trading broker. When you make a search online, you will easily find different brokers who will offer you their services. With so many brokers to choose from, how can you tell the one that will best suit your needs as a trader? Here are the criteria to look for:

- Latest ratings and reviews

Before you start depositing money into your trading account, it is wise for you to check the latest ratings and reviews that other traders have given your broker. It is easy to do this. Just use your favorite browser and type the name of your broker, and then add the word "reviews." The search engine results page (SERP) will then give a list of related pages. Read as many reviews as you can about your broker. It is a common practice for brokers to hire writers to come up with positive write-ups about them, so do not rely on a single website or review. Also take note of the cons that other traders share about a particular broker. You should also pay attention to the dates when the latest reviews were made. If the last review was made about a year ago, then you should exercise caution. Do not forget that brokers may change how they run the business, and even the people who manage the business can also change. It is of utmost importance that you work with a reliable broker, so take as much time as you need in choosing a good broker. Another good way to find a good broker is by joining and participating in online groups and forums on forex trading.

- Customer support

Make sure that your broker has an active customer support. In the course of being a trader, there will most likely come a time when you will have to contact your broker's customer support to deal with some issues, whether technical issues or otherwise. Any questions that you may have regarding the trading platform, technical problems, or in managing your account, can be directed to the customer support team. For example, if you have problems with your latest withdrawal, then you will have to contact the customer support team for help. This is how important the customer support is. A good way to know if a broker has a good customer support is by testing it. To do this, simply send a message to the customer support and inquire about something. A good question would be to ask for any substitute documents that you may submit when making a withdrawal. It is common for brokers to require traders to send some identity before processing a withdrawal. Pay attention to how fast and professional the customer support team responds and resolves your inquiry.

A broker may offer several ways to contact the customer support team. Most brokers will provide you with an on-page contact form and also an email address. Others may also have a live chat support. Normally, the live chat support follows a schedule, so be sure to take note of the time when it will be open. Also check if there is a phone number that you can contact. If there is, try to contact the number just to see if it is working. Needless to say, you should only work with a broker that has an excellent and professional customer support. Surely, in the life of a trader, you will have to rely on your broker's customer support team from time to time.

- Trading platform

Your broker should provide you with enough tools to help you come up with a sound trading decision. It must, at the least, provide you with the graphs that you will need for technical analysis. The more tools and information that your broker gives you for free, the better. The trading platform should also be professionally designed and easy to navigate. This means that it should have a simple yet professional layout that will allow you to use the platform easily and conveniently. Making a trade should be as fast and easy as doing a few clicks of a mouse. The trading tools and other important pages should also be easily accessible. Keep in mind that the trading platform is what you will use for trading so it should at least be properly set up in a way that will encourage you to be ina professional mood to do your trades. The combination of colors and the overall design should be easy on the eyes. Simply put, the trading platform should make the activity of trading easier and more convenient for you.

- Transaction cost

Check the transaction cost that your broker imposes for every trade that you make. Normally, there will no longer be any separate transaction cost since a broker will already make a profit from the *spread*. However, some brokers make money on a commission basis where they get a certain percentage of the spread. Hence, find out if the broker is going to impose its transaction cost on per spread basis or on commission. Also check if the broker imposes other fees every transaction. These days, most brokers only charge based on the spread involved in a trade.

- Banking methods

Before you deposit any money into your trading account, you should check the banking methods/options offered by your broker. It is not uncommon to find brokers that offer more options for making a deposit than for making a withdrawal. The problem here is that you risk having your money locked out in your account without any way of making a withdrawal. Therefore, be sure that the banking options given by your broker allow you to make a deposit, as well as a withdrawal. Another thing that you should take note of is the requirements that you need to meet before your broker processes a withdrawal, especially when making your first withdrawal. Most brokers will require you to submit some identity documents, such as a valid ID and a proof of billing with your address. Make sure that you have these documents available in your possession. If not, then contact your broker's customer support team and ask if you could submit other documents. It is important that you get this one clear before you even deposit any money into your account.

When making a deposit, a broker would rarely ask you for anything that you will need to comply with except to fund your account using their offered deposit options. However, when making a withdrawal, this is usually where the problem occurs as many brokers will ask you to comply with some requirements. It is not uncommon to find traders who have not been paid by their broker after requesting for a withdrawal. Make sure that you only work with a legitimate and reliable broker. If you work with a legitimate broker, then you will surely get your money provided that you meet your broker's withdrawal requirements. In a way, this is unfair in the sense that there is no issue at all when making a deposit but lots of issues when making a withdrawal. Come to think of it, when you make a deposit, you do fund your account but the numbers that appear in your trading account is not the money that you just deposited. They are just numbers on the screen. The money that you deposited is received by your broker. As long as you do not make a successful withdrawal, then all that you have would be numbers on a screen, as if you were using a demo account. It is only when you make a successful withdrawal when a broker has to release real money – the money that is rightfully yours. Once again, it is worth stressing that it is of primary importance that you only work with a trustworthy and legitimate broker.

- Deposit and withdrawal limit

It is also good to know the rules of your broker in terms of the deposit and withdrawal amount. Find out the minimum deposit and the maximum deposit that you can make per day, as well as the minimum and maximum withdrawal limit. The minimum requirement and maximum limits vary from broker to broker. If this information is not found on your broker's website under the *banking* or *FAQ* page, then send an inquiry to the customer support team.

- Currency pairs available

Not all brokers offer the same number of currency pairs. Of course, the more there are currency pairs offered by your broker, the more choices that you will have. Your broker must at least have the major currency pairs, such as the EUR/USD, USD/JPY, USD/CHF, and GBP/USD. Of course, traders may also have a certain interest in a particular currency pair which may not even be considered as a major currency pair. In such case, the important thing is for your broker to offer the currency pair that you are interested in. Remember that a good broker will make the experience of trading currencies easy and more convenient and not the other way around.

- Bonuses and promotions

It is normal for forex brokers to offer bonuses and promotions. For example, if you deposit $200 in your trading account, you will get an additional $50 that you can trade.

This means that you will have $250 in your account. However, be careful before you accept a bonus or promo. Usually, this kind of bonus has some drawbacks attached to it. After all, no broker would give you free money just for nothing. Do not expect for brokers to give out money just for the purpose of being kind to you. Keep in mind that when you engage in forex trading, everything is pure business. So, what is the catch? The catch is that, usually, when you accept a bonus or promo, you will not be able to withdraw your money until you meet the requirement imposed by your broker. Normally, this may take the form of having to trade up to 50 times the bonus that you received or at least be able to reach a certain profit but which is too high for your initial investment. Hence, in the case of a $50 bonus, then you will have to trade up to the amount of $2,500 so you can withdraw the bonus money. Most traders will be wiped out before they even reach the broker's wagering requirements. Also, since the traders will be compelled to reach the requirement, they tend to be aggressive in their approach which further increases their chances of losing all their investment. Kindly take note that this is only an example. Your broker may impose a different kind of requirement. Therefore, remember: Before you accept a bonus or promo, make sure that you read the terms and conditions that are attached to it. If the terms are not clear enough, do not hesitate to contact the customer support team. If you think that the terms are not fair, then you are free not to accept the offer.

Important Information for US-Based Traders

If you are a trader who is based is based in the U.S., there are certain things that you should take note of. As you may already know by now, there are brokers out there who do not accept traders who reside in the U.S. Now, some people may still be able to find a way to use the services of a broker without revealing that they reside in the U.S.; however, it is advised that you respect a broker's policy and just stay away from it. The truth is that FX brokers are not stupid. They may allow you to deposit money and even make many trades but they can start to give you problems once you request for a withdrawal. Since you are the one who intentionally violated the terms, then there is almost nothing that you can do about it. In fact, a broker will most probably be able to terminate your account. Also, even if you use TOR to hide your residence, do not expect to be able to fool your broker. There are other ways that your broker can do to find out your real location. So, to be safe, stay away from brokers who do not welcome U.S. traders.

Although the FX market is decentralized, it does not mean

that brokers are also not regulated properly. In the U.S., all trustworthy and legitimate brokers are a member of the National Futures Association (NFA) and also registered with the U.S. Commodity Futures Trading Commission (CFTC). Membership in the NFA is required in the U.S. for all those who participate in the futures market, including forex brokers. The purpose of CFTC is to "protect market users and the public from fraud, manipulation and abusive practices related to the sale of commodity and financial futures and options, and to foster open, competitive and financially-sound futures and option markets." You can easily find out if your broker is associated to these regulatory bodies by visiting your broker's website. Normally, you will find this information in the About Us page of your broker's website. Do not be fooled by the design of a broker's website. A professionally-designed website does not guarantee that the broker has met the regulatory compliance. Steer clear from brokers who are not associated with the National Futures Association and the Commodity Futures Trading Commission.

CHAPTER 4: FOREX TRADING STRATEGIES

You cannot expect to make continuous profits by trading foreign currencies if you just rely on luck. Actively participating in the forex market for a long term can be a daunting task. In fact, there is no amount of preparation and research that can guarantee that a particular position will give you a positive profit. However, there are strategies that you can use that can significantly increase your chances of success. Although you can still expect to experience some losses every now and then, these strategies can help turn the odds in your favor and allow you to end up with a positive profit in the long run.

- Fundamental Analysis

This analysis is sometimes referred to as the *lifeblood of investment* for good reasons. As its name suggests, fundamental analysis deals with the fundamentals or the basics. Take note that *basics* does not mean that it is composed of elements that are easy to understand. Rather, *basics* refer to the very foundation of things. In forex trading, this involves knowing and analyzing fundamental indicators to see if a particular currency is undervalued or overvalued relative to another currency. Fundamental analysis also analyzes the different factors or elements that affect the prices of the different currencies. An important part of fundamental analysis is to be updated in the news. In fact, some people refer to fundamental analysis as news analysis since this approach is primarily concerned about being updated on the news and analyzing it. When you apply fundamental analysis, the step is to be aware of the news that may have an effect upon the prices of different currencies, especially those that may affect the currencies that you want to trade. Keep in mind that there are many factors that can influence the price of a currency, such as the economy, technological developments, market acceptance and use, the level of competition, government relations and regulations, and businesses, among other things. So, for example, if you read in a newspaper that there is underemployment in the United States, and all other things being equal, then there is a good chance that the price of the U.S. dollar can decrease. Once you know this, then you can take appropriate actions to take advantage of it. You should also check the record of the currency inflows and outflows. This is published b the central bank. Of course, when you use fundamental analysis, you are expected to spend lots of time doing research and analysis.

As a professional trader, fundamental analysis should be a part of your life. When it come to the forex market, the amount and quality of information that you have play a crucial role since trading decisions are based on what you know about the market. Hence, the more that you understand the market, the more that you will be able to come up with a sound investment decision. Fundamental analysis is also a strategy that you can combine with other strategies, such as technical analysis. Keep in mind that knowing the basics is important. In fact, many of the changes that occur in the prices of different currencies can easily be explained just by understanding the basics or the fundamentals.

- Technical Analysis

If you are more of a visual person, then you might want to learn technical analysis. Most traders use this strategy due to its effectiveness and simplicity. If you think that fundamental analysis is too tiring, then technical analysis combines everything altogether that all that you need to do is to analyze graphs and charts. The concept behind this strategy is that all of the factors or elements that affect the different currencies have their final effect upon the price. Therefore, by simply analyzing the price movements of the different currencies as shown by the graphs, you get to deal with all the said elements. After all, regardless of what is happening in the world, the only thing that truly matters is how the prices of the currencies move in the market. If you are able to predict their movements, then you can easily take appropriate actions and earn a decent profit.

The key to technical analysis is to be able to read patterns. Yes, patterns do exist. In fact, if you allow a random generator to play for some time, it will also create some patterns. It is worth remembering that patterns come and go. Therefore, do not expect to see a pattern every time that you look at a graph. A common problem with traders who use technical analysis is that they force to see a pattern even when it does not really exist. Do not delude yourself. Keep in mind that you are not obliged to enter a trade. Therefore, only make a trade when you see a good opportunity to profit. Just because you have spent about an hour or two analyzing a pattern does not mean that you should make a decision to trade right away. When you use technical analysis, patience is an important virtue that you should learn. Now, in the event that you identify a pattern, then you should act quickly and take advantage of it.

Technical analysis is definitely one of the strategies that you should learn as a trader. It is also not uncommon to see traders who use this strategy with another strategy. Once you learn how to *read* graphs and charts, you will easily be able to draw information simply by looking at them. Hence, no matter what strategy you use, you can always use your skill in reading charts to help you come up with a better trading decision. Once again, the more information and understanding that you have about a particular currency or currencies, the more likely that you will be able to predict their movement. Needless to say, this kind of knowledge is something that you can turn into a profit.

- Scalping

If you would rather have small but consistent profit, then you should learn scalping. Since the potential profit is small, your risk will also be small. Of course, the key to profit with this strategy is having multiple small profits. Therefore, as a scalper, you need to be patient and diligent at the same time. If you are the type of trader who only wants to profit a big amount quickly, then this is not for you. Basically, scalping is where you enter a position and then leave it the moment that you realize a profit. Hence, this strategy is perfect for day traders. An important element of scalping is identifying the currency pair to invest in. Some traders merely rely on the volatility that is inherent in the forex market. However, it is worth noting that merely relying on volatility is not good enough. Instead, you need to rely on the hard facts and actual details. Therefore, as a trader, you are expected to do as much research as possible to help you develop your own understanding of the market.

When you use scalping, you should keep a close eye on the market while your position is open. All you need is a small profit, and then you should close your position. It is an excellent short-term strategy. Another important element of scalping is to know when to close your position. It can be very tempting to continuously hold a position, especially when you are profiting from it. However, keep in mind that holding on to a position for a longer time also increases your risk. After all, the fact remains that no matter how profitable a position may be, the market can still suddenly fall at any time. When you use scalping, you should minimize your risk as much as possible. Do not worry; if your position is truly profitable, you can still get back to it. The important thing about scalping is to be able to profit a little by risking also a little. Do not be greedy. Scalping is effective, but it takes time and you will have to do it many times to earn a significant amount of profit.

A notable disadvantage of using scalping is that it requires a large deposit; otherwise, the profit that you will get per successful trade would be almost negligible. If you do not invest a big amount, then you would earn very little even after ten successful trades using scalping.

- Momentum trading

The key to this strategy is to identify strong price movements.

The idea behind this strategy is that a strong price movement that is headed towards a particular direction is most likely going to continue for some more time. After all, the fluctuation caused by a strong price movement cannot be expected to counterbalance itself quickly. Momentum trading usually uses the same graphs and charts used in technical analysis since it deals directly with the price movements of a currency pair. Since momentum trading only aims to take advantage of the momentum of a strong price movement by following its direction, it is only suitable for short-term trading. This strategy is actually easy to use. You simply need to spot a strong price movement and take advantage of it before the trend changes.

Another important part of momentum trading is knowing when to close your position. It can sometimes be very tempting to hold your position and hope for the momentum to last longer. The problem is that by the time you realize that the momentum has already stopped, your profits might have already turned into losses. Therefore, in order to avoid this from happening, you should avoid getting greedy. The key is to exit the momentum trade even before it stops. Now, there is no hard and fast rule as to how you can determine up to how long a momentum trade is going to last. To be safe, just aim for a small profit and exit the position once you hit it. Do not forget that this strategy is about taking advantage of the momentum, which means that a strong price movement has already taken place, so do not hold on to the position for too long.

- Swing trading

Swing trading is a long-term trading strategy. As a swing trader, you should expect to experience multiple price fluctuations. This is norm on the forex market, especially if you hold a position for a long period. A good thing about being a swing trader is that you can earn a high amount of profit by the time that you close your position. Another advantage of using this strategy is that you do not have to study the market every day. Although it is still advised that you at least check on the market on a daily basis. This is just to ensure that your position is not being compromised. From time to time, you at see that you are losing the trade, but do not panic. Again, you should expect for some price fluctuations to take place. The important thing is to be in a profitable position when you exit the trade. Hence, do not allow yourself to be affected by the day-to-day volatility of the forex market for such is bound to happen.

Of course, you cannot expect to make a profit simply by holding on to a particular position for a long term. It is still important for you to choose the right currency to invest in. How you pick a currency depends on you. You may use financial analysis, technical analysis, or any other approach that you prefer. Unlike momentum trading where you normally just aim for a small profit, swing trading usually brings a significant amount of profit since it has a much longer trading period. The drawback is that this is also the style of trading that can lead to a serious loss since it involves holding your position for a long time. Although swing traders usually ignore the day-to-day fluctuations in price even in the case of a loss, these fluctuations can easily pile ofup over time and turn into a significant amount. This is also an excellent strategy to use for part-time traders as you do not have to follow the market regularly. Most swing traders only make a few trades in a month. The key is to focus on the quality of the trade than on quantity.

- Hedging

Simply put, hedging is a way to protect yourself against a big loss. Consider it as an insurance in case something unexpected happens that can adversely affect you as a trader. There are brokers that will allow you to hedge directly where you can purchase a currency pair and at the same time place place a trade to sell the said pair. Although youaynot have a net profit while both trades are open, you can earn more without taking on addition risk if you observe proper timing. The way a hedge protects you is by allowing you to open anopposite trade while you are also trading the same currency pair. Of course, as a trader, you are free to just close your initial trade and then move to a new trade. A good thing about hedging is that you can save your trade and even make money if the market suddenly moves against your initial position. Now, in case the market reverses and takes a direction that is favorable to your first trade/position, then you can place a stop on the hedging trade or simply close it. This is the simplest way of hedging.

It is worth noting that hedging is not suggested tobe used bybeginners. Its proper application requires adequate knowledge of the market, price swings, and proper timing.

- Scaling in

Scaling in is where you enter a trade little by little or in pieces instead of putting everything in one position all at once. A trader who is looking to scale in may want to divide his position into quarters or in any way he deems best. Scaling in is an effective way to control your risk as you get to have a better understanding of how the market moves.

For example, if the total amount that you are willing to invest in a trade is $200, you divide it in half (or in quarters or in any way that you want) to start scaling in. Let us say that you open a position and invest $100, if the position turns out to be favorable, then you realize a profit. It is now up to you whether you still want to add the other $100. Now, let us assume that after adding the other $100, the price movement reverses and you start to lose the trade, since you have an initial investment at a much lower cost and has already profited, then you will be able to lower your total losses. Of course, the drawback here is that in the vent that the trade continues to be profitable, you will not earn as much as if you just invested the whole $200 at once on the first trade. Still, this strategy is worth learning since it effectively lowers your risk. As you may already know, being too aggressive is not a suggested approach as it can exhaust your funds quickly. To stay longer in the market and remain profitable, you need to control your risk and minimize your losses.

- Scaling out

If scaling in is about adding and having more open positions, scaling out is about lowering your exposure to risk by closing out some of your positions. Hence, this is the opposite of scaling in. Let us say that you are very confident about a certain trade and so you make a big investment into it. However, as time goes by, you realize that it is starting not to be as profitable as you have thought. This usually happens when a news piece that can have a negative impact on a trade gets featured. Suddenly, you start to feel less confident of your trade; however you still think that it can still be profitable. Now, since you find it hard to predict how the market will respond and are now quite unsure of the profitability of your position, you can start scaling out by closing some of your positions or lowering your invested amount in a trade. This way you can still profit if the market turns out to be favorable; however, in case that the market becomes unfavorable, then scaling out would be able to cut back your losses effectively.

So, how do you know when to scale in and when to scale out?

This depends on how you think the market will move. If you predict that the market will move favorably, then scaling in would be the better option. However, if you become unsure of the profitability of your position, then scaling out would be the better option. In a volatile market where your position earns a profit but you are aware that it will soon take a downhill, scaling out will allow you to continuously take advantage of the current price movement with a much lower risk.

- Averaging down

Averaging down is an effective way to invest in a currency pair at a bargain price. It is also a good way to earn a high amount of profit. However, it is considered an aggressive approach, so be cautious of using this strategy. The key to this strategy is to identify as currency pair that you think would be profitable in the near future. You then invest in that currency pair. Let us say that the price drops and you experience some losses, instead of closing your position, you should make another investment in the same currency pair. Since the price has also dropped, then the cost of the pair will now also be lower. Continue to do this as the price of the currency pair decreases. Okay, although this may seem like a losing strategy at first, it can actually turn out to be highly profitable after some time. Just imagine what will happen if its price finally reverses and increases back either to its original value when you first applied this strategy, or higher. As you can see, all your open positions will experience a nice profit. This is an effective and highly profitable strategy. The important thing is to be able to identify a currency pair that would be profitable in the near future and then hold on to it. To do this, you may want to research as much as you can about the currencies involved in a pair, so that you can have a better understanding of how likely their prices are going to change in the next few days or weeks. Although this strategy seems very practical and highly profitable, it is noteworthy that you should be very careful in using this approach. If you fail to pick a profitable currency pair, then you will most likely lose a lot of money. Use this strategy with caution. Be sure to follow on the market and stay updated on the latest news that may be relevant to your investment/trade.

- Pin bar strategy

This is a strategy that you can apply when you are using technical analysis. You can easily identify the right time to use this strategy by looking at a graph. The signal is when you see a horizontal line which means that the price fluctuations have been stagnant over some time. This horizontal line is what is referred to as the *bullish pin bar*. The concept behind this theory is that the resistance will serve as a new support for a price increase. Hence, if you make an investment at any point in the bullish pin bar, then you will most likely experience a profit in the very near future. Hence, when you see a bullish pin bar, you should consider entering the market and opening a position depending on the currency pair where it applies. Take note that this does not work 100% of the time. However, there is a good chance that it will turn out to be a good investment. A better approach is to spot for a bullish pin bar and make some more research before investing your money in a trade. This way you will be more confident and also increase your chances of making the right trading decision.

- Forex wedge breakout

There are many breakout strategies. With this one, what you are looking for is a wedge pattern where the price goes up and down. However, unlike a usually wedge, you will see that the differences between the price increase and decrease gets smaller over time. You will know that if the pattern continues then it will soon to an end and become a mere horizontal line. The key is to take advantage of this pattern before it disappears. So, you should open a position just immediately after a price decrease. Keep in mind that you should not hold on to the position for so long; otherwise, you will more likely experience a bad loss. To be safe, stay conservative. Once you make a profit by a few pips, close down your position. How much you will profit will depend on the behavior of the pattern, but it will most likely be lower than the previous increase in value. Be sure to take advantage of this opportunity and close your position while still at a profit.

- Retracement

The concept behind this strategy is that prices do not move in a straight line especially during highs and lows. Instead, they usually make a pause or only change in the middle of a larger path. Hence, when you apply retracement, you will wait for the price to "retrace" itself or pull back. This is to confirm that a pattern is being made. Once you are able to identify this, then you can make use of the pattern that is being formed by taking appropriate actions. When trading currencies, knowing the most probable movement of the price in a graph is a big advantage that can lead to profit.

- Reversal trading

As its name already suggests, this is where you expected a reversal in the price trend, and your objective here is to make an entrance into a trade that is ahead of the market. This is not really a strategy for beginners as it requires you to have more understanding of how the market moves. Reversals do not always occur but they can be highly profitable if you are able to take advantage of them. There are tools that traders use in order to identify a reversal, such as visual cues, as well as volume and momentum indicators.

- Go with the flow

Sometimes the best way to trade is simply to go with the flow. The key to this is simply to be updated on the news. If the US economy is doing really well, then you may want to start going long on it, especially if the economy of the other currency is not showing any development. You simply have to see which one is going strong in the market. You can also apply this using technical analysis. If you see a strong price movement, then you can take advantage of it. Still, when you use this approach, no matter what strategy you use, you should apply fundamental analysis in order to significantly increase your chances of making a profit. If you do not want to make any research, you might want to read the posts on forex trading forums and see how the traders respond. Sometimes you may be able to spot interesting ideas and profitable opportunities. However, just make sure not to rely completely on whatever you read from other people. It is still important for you to develop your own understanding of the forex market.

- Conservative

This strategy simply encourages that you should be conservative in your approach. Avoid trades that are aggressive, especially those that lack sufficient research. The key to this approach is to make small but multiple trades. Instead of focusing on how much you can earn from every trade, you should focus on increasing your rate of success. The idea behind this approach is that once you are able to establish an effective strategy, then you can always increase the amount that you trade with. As a beginner, what is important is for you to work on a powerful strategy that can give you a high rate of success. Be as conservative as possible and never commence a trade that uses more than 5% of your total funds. The key is to stay low and let your small yet continuous gains turn into a significant profit. Also, by remaining conservative, you will not be provoked to turn into an emotional trader. This is also an excellent strategy to stay longer in the market. It is also strongly suggested if it is your first time to trade in a real forex market using real money. Be as conservative as possible and cut back on your risks and losses. Last but not least, keep your focus on making continuous small profits. Being consistent is the key. Once you are able to establish a good flow of profits and if you are already confident enough in your strategy, then that is the time for you to increase the amount that you invest per trade. Still, be sure not to use more than 5% of your total funds per trade.

- Copy trade

Some brokers have a copy trade feature. What this does is to copy the trades of other traders. Of course, it is you who will choose the trader whose trades you want to copy. Needless to say, when you use this strategy, you need to identify an experienced and successful trader among the majority of traders who either earn a little or even lose their investment. Be sure to check the profile page of a trader and take a look at his success rate. Also find out about his current open positions and analyze it. Again, having your own understanding of the market is important.

If you are able to spot a really skillful and successful trader, then all it takes is a few clicks of a mouse to follow and copy all his trades.

Another way of using copy trade is by plotting the trades and success rate of a certain trader. You will not find a trader with 100% success rate, except if he is a new trader who has not yet encountered any losses. The trick here is to track his trades and only join him if you think that his trade is going to be successful. By doing this, you can "skip" the trades that will most probably not turn out favorably. You should be careful about this as it is not easy to predict when a certain trader will lose in a trade. A good way to apply this is by making your own analysis of the situation. It should be noted that although there are some people who are already happy just by copying other people's trading decisions, it is still advised that you, as a professional trader, should not copy a trade just for the sake of copying. You will not grow as a trader if all that you do is copy another person's trades.

- Make your own

Although there are many strategies that you can find about forex trading, the best approach is still for you to device your own strategy. After all, different circumstances may require a different approach. You must adapt a strategy that is both effective and flexible. You are also free to modify already existing strategies, but you can also come up with something that is completely of your own invention. It does not really matter what strategy you use, what is important is if it is effective enough to yield into profits. A strategy also does not have to be complicated to be effective. After all, as you already know by now, trading currencies is not a complicated activity. Mostly, it is just about identifying the right currency to invest in. It is just about predicting whether the value of a particular currency will increase or decrease against the other currency in its pair.

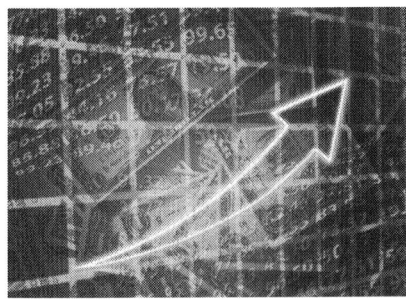

Do not expect to develop your own strategy quickly. It takes time to come up with an effective strategy. To test just how effective your strategy is, you should test it many times in a live market and see how it performs. Strategies also change over time just as the market also changes. Hence, professional traders are known for always working on their strategy.

CHAPTER 5: BEST PRACTICES

- Insufficient research

It is true that more than 90% of forex traders do some research before they enter any position. However, it is also true that majority of these traders do not do sufficient amount of research. Take note that when it comes to trading foreign currencies, the amount and quality of information that you have matter. If you do not have sufficient information, how do you think you can come up with a sound investment decision? Also, do not think that doing research for two hours is already enough research. I am telling you, many traders do the same thing but then end up losing their money. As stated in the previous chapter, fundamental analysis should be a part of your day-to-day activity as a trader. Never enter a trade when you are not confident of your understanding of the market. Remember that you are not obliged to make a trade. However, when you do, make sure that you take a profitable position. Of course, there is no amount of preparation or research that can completely guarantee any profit, but the more information that you have, the easier it will be for you to make a sound trading decision.

Do not just learn about the market; you should also be open to how other traders react to the market and apply their strategy. Do not forget that market reaction, including how traders respond to changes, can affect the prices of different currencies. It is also suggested that you join and participate in online group and forums on forex trading. There are also interesting lessons and updates that you can learn from there. When you work as a forex trader, sometimes having additional information can make a big difference. Do not worry; you are not competing with other traders. In fact, if you give it a try, you will most probably learn a lot from other traders. But then again, do not rely on other people's opinions. As we have already discussed, you should strive to have your own understanding ofof the market. Of course, having your own understanding does not mean closing your doors to opportunities toand other ways to gather more information about the market.

- Keeping a trading journal or diary

It is not required for you to write a trading journal. However, having a journal can be very beneficial. It will allow you to view yourself from a different perspective without any bias or prejudice. Do not worry; you do not need to be a professional writer to have a trading journal. However, you need to update your journal regularly and be honest with everything that you write in it. Your trading journal should serve as a mirror of yourself as a trader, so that by reading your journal, you will be more able to understand yourself as a trader.

So, what should you write in your journal? You can write anything and everything that is related to forex trading. Again, remember to update it regularly and be honest with everything that you write. Ideally, your journal should include your reasons for trading. Also write down your goals and objectives as a trader. This may help you someday if ever you feel lost in your journey as a forex trader. Remember that you can always come back to this page in your journal, and it will give you a sense of direction. You should also write the strategies that you are using and those that you want to learn. Your journal should also containa record of all your trades. Needlessto say, you should also read your journal from time to time. It is not uncommon to see improvements that you can still make to your strategy and even to yourself as a trader just by reading your journal. As a trader, committing mistakes is part of the learning process. Make sure to include them in your trading journal. As you can see, a trading journal can help you become a better trader by helping you understand yourself.

It is suggested that you use a notebook as your trading journal. However, you can also use a word file on your computer. Just be sure not to lose it. There are also many writing applications that you can download and run on your mobile phone. The important thing is to make your journal easily accessible, so that it will not be hard for you to update and/or read it. Although you are not required to keep a journal, there is no doubt that the benefits that you can get from it can be extremely valuable.

- Do not chase after your losses

Even in casino gambling, it is a common rule not to chase after your losses. The reason is that if you do, then you will most likely lose your money. Of course, you can still get lucky and be able to recover your losses quickly; however, you cannot expect for this kind of strategy to work in the long run. In the long run, there more than 90% that you will end up with lots of losses if you continue chasing after your losses. Chasing after your losses will only give you more losses to chase until you go bankrupt. Although chasing after your losses can be very tempting to do, you need to exercise self-control. Instead, what you should do is to focus on chasing more profits.

Chasing after your losses will only compel you to turn aggressive. The problem with a highly aggressive approach is that you expose yourself to too much risk. As a professional trader, it is your responsibility to manage your risks. Another problem with chasing after your losses is that there is almost no room for error since you will be using a higher percentage of your total funds in order to increase your potential profit. Some even chase their losses and go as far as placing all their funds in a single trading position. The problem here is that, sometimes, losing a trade is inevitable. Again. The best solution is simply to accept your losses and just focus on chasing after more profits.

- Do not be an emotional trader

Allowing your emotions to get in the way and cloud your judgment can be very dangerous for you as a trader. The forex market means business. It is not going to care whether or not make any money. In fact, it would not care about you even if you lose all your money in a single day. The forex market moves on and continues no matter what you do. Although it is good for you to have passion in what you do, never allow this passion to control your thinking. The forex market is all about money and business, so stay objective at all times. If you suddenly feel that you are being emotional, then stop and give yourself time to calm down and relax. A good way to avoid being an emotional trader is by investing only the money that you can afford to lose. This way you will not be very much attached to the money that you use for trading. It is hard to enjoy trading if you knowthat the money that you are using is the money that you need to pay for your house rent or electric bill. Therefore, always remember to spend only the money that you can afford to lose.

Of course, this does not mean that positive emotions like feeling very inspired are a bad thing. In fact, you should get as much inspiration as you can. After all, the path of a forex trader is a long and challenging path. Nonetheless, it is a path that is worth taking for it can definitely change your life for the better. As a professional forex trader, you should keep watch of your emotions. If you notice that you emotions are starting to dominate your way of thinking, then just stop. Sometimes the best way to deal with a strong emotion is by being inactive. If you give it enough time, it will subside and disappear on its own.

You should also avoid getting too sentimental. Some traders forget to be objective and just continue to hold onto a particular position for sentimental reasons. Take note that there is no sentimentality in the forex market. You enter and exit a position for good reasons and mainly to get a profit. It is all about making a profit. Therefore, no matter how much you may like a particular currency pair, if such position is no longer profitable enough, then it is time for you to abandon it. Conversely, even if you do not like a particular currency, if all indicators point to it as the most profitable option, then you should grab the opportunity right away. As you can see, there is no use being emotional when you deal with the forex market. After all, the life of a forex trader is the kind of life where nobody cares about you. You make your own decisions and you face all the consequences of your actions. Hence, you need to be very careful, and the best way to be careful is to use your mind and think objectively.

- Diversify

You are probably aware of the saying that "You should not put all your eggs in one basket." The same is true when you engage in FX trading. Instead of opening a big position where you have invested all your funds, it would be better to open multiple smaller positions. After all, as you already know by now, no matter how much preparation you make, there is no 100% guarantee that a particular trade will turn out to be profitable. You can only increase your chances of choosing a profitable trade but you cannot be certain about it. Diversifying would require you to do more research and analysis, but it is an effective way to minimize your risk.

- Continuous practice

Learning to trade currencies profitably requires continuous practice. In fact, if you are just starting out, it is well advised that you do not focus on making money right away. Instead, you should first familiarize yourself with the actual trading environment. This is a good time to take advantage of the demo account provided by your broker. Beginners are also encouraged to start out small regardless of the amount of their funds that they may have in their account.

You should keep on working on your trading strategy. The forex market is a continuously moving market. Therefore, you can expect that you will have to modify your strategy from time to time to keep it effective.

It can be said that your whole journey as a trader is one long practice. There is simply no end to self-development. The important thing is to be open to it and take positive actions to improve yourself. Before you apply any strategy, it is important that you give yourself enough time to practice and have mastery of a certain strategy. While you are applying the said strategy, you are still expected to study it and find ways to make it better. As you can see, there is no end to improving one's craft. In fact, there are known strategies today that merely came from experiments through trial and error.

You need to keep on practicing in order to keep on learning, so that you can grow as a trader. There are some parts of being a trader that you cannot learn just by reading books. Many times, you will need to have an actual experience, and the only way to do this is by engaging in actual practice.

- Have a plan

Have a plan before you enter any kind of trade. As a rule, you should have a short-term plan and a long-term plan. This is to prepare you for contingencies that may occur in the market. It is not uncommon for a short-term trade to suddenly turn into a long-term trade. In the same way, a long-term trade can suddenly be cut short, depending on the circumstances in the market. Therefore, it is suggested that you should always have a plan when you enter a trade. Having a plan will ensure your sense of direction over the course of a trade and not lose of your objective. For your short-term plan, ask yourself by how many pips you intend to profit. Once you reach your target, you should be discipline enough to close your position before the market takes a different direction. Of course, in some instances, it is wise to continue to hold on to your position. This is where having a long-term plan will be handy. The same is true if you start with a long-term plan. Sometimes, certain events may happen that it would no longer be a good choice to cling to your long-term plan. In this case, you will have to cut it short in order to avoid losing your money in the trade. Remember to always have a plan and never lose sight of your objective.

- Take a break

The life of a forex trader, especially if you are a day trader, can be exhausting. You should make it a priority to give yourself time to relax from time to time. Do not worry; the market will keep on moving even when you get back to it. After all, you do not have to follow every second of its movement. It is simply in the nature of the forex market to keep on moving. By giving yourself enough time to take a break, you will be able to rest your body and clear your mind. Know that you will be a more effective trader if only you allow your mind to take some rest. Some traders feel guilty about giving themselves a chance to relax, and that is wrong. Remember: Taking a break is part of the journey.

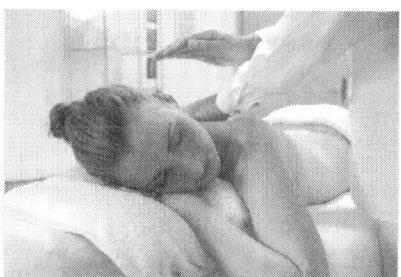

When you allow yourself to rest, you should do something that will completely take your mind off of trading. Some traders take a break but still think of their trades. That is not a good way to relax. When you take a break, it is also important that you do not think about forex trading at all. It is a good opportunity for you to go to the beach and enjoy a vacation with your family. Enjoy it as much as you can. Know that after taking a break, you are expected to focus more on your work as a trader.

Taking a break is not an excuse for being lazy. Normally, you only give yourself a chance to take a break *after* spending a serious time with work. It is also good to give yourself a treat from time to time. After all, you do not work as a trader just for the sake of working. You should also enjoy the fruits of your labor. Take a break and enjoy life.

- Cash out

Some traders have the habit of not making any withdrawal. The reason is that they want to grow their funds. After all, the more money you have that you can trade, the more profit that you can make. Although this may seem reasonable and logical, you should also understand that it is only by cashing out that you are truly able to experience the fruit of your labor. If you do not cash out, then it is just like using a demo account. The thing is that you do not have to cash out all your money or winnings at once. If you want, you can request for a withdrawal f just around 10% of your weekly profit. The important thing is that you make a successful withdrawal, and be sure not to send that money back into your account. Also, by making a withdrawal, you get to lower your risk since the money that is withdrawn can no longer be lost as it is already outside of your investment. This ensures that you get to keep or use the money that you withdraw. As long as the money stays in your trading account or is invested in something, then there is always the risk that you may lose it. Therefore, make it a priority to cash out from time to time. How many times you cash out and when you make a withdrawal would depend on your style of trading. If you are a day trader, then requesting for a withdrawal once a week or every two weeks may be a good choice. For long-term trades, then you may want to request for a withdrawal after closing a particular trade where you earn a high profit.

- Professional approach

Many people who jump into forex trading usually approach it as a hobby. Although there is nothing wrong with taking forex trading as a hobby, it is not the suggested way to deal with the forex market. The reason is that if you only approach it as a hobby, then you will most likely get what you deserve from it.

You may only earn a small amount or even lose all your investment. This is because having continuous success in the forex market requires so much more than treating it as a mere hobby. Many professional and successful traders spend hours every day just to come up with a sound trading decision; and yet, from time to time, they still lose a trade. In order to increase your chances of success, you should approach the forex market professionally. Treat it as a business or a formal profession. This means that you should also exercise discipline and be committed to it. You should also dedicate to it enough time and effort; otherwise, you will only be relying on luck just like any other gambler. Unfortunately, considering how the forex market is designed, it is obvious that it is not made for those people who merely rely on luck to succeed.

- Connect with like-minded people

Life as a forex trader can sometimes get lonely. After all, this is the kind of career where you are completely on your own. You enjoy your profits alone, but you also suffer losses on your own. There is no one in the forex market whom you can depend on to comfort you. Therefore, it is also good if you connect with like-minded people. Feel free to make friends with other traders. After all, you are all players in the market who want the same thing. The good thing is that you are not competing with one another. In fact, you can even help one another by sharing information, insights, and strategies. Thanks to the Internet, it is very easy to find and connect with people who are also interested in forex trading. You simply have to join an online group or forum on forex trading. You can do this quickly with just a few clicks of a mouse. You can then make a public post or even send a private message to any member of the group/forum. If you have a neighbor or friend who also likes trading currencies, then you can invite him out for a coffee one of these days. Connecting with like-minded people is not just a way to learn but it can also inspire you to become a better trader.

- Have fun

Forex trading is fun. This is a fact. In fact, many traders get to enjoy this kind of life that they still continue to learn it despite their losses. It is also not uncommon to find traders, especially beginners, who spend their whole day just learning about forex trading. Like gambling in a casino, trading currencies can also be very addicting, especially if you are making a nice profit from it.

Learn to have fun and enjoy the journey. Sometimes taking

things too seriously can ruin the experience and even make you less effective. In your life as a trader, you will definitely make some mistakes from time to time. You will experience losing money from what otherwise would have been a profitable trade if only you knew better. Do not get too stressed. The important thing is for you to learn as much as you can from every mistake. Take it easy, but remember to learn from the experience. Making mistakes is part of the learning process. Of course, you should try to minimize them as much as possible. Learn and have fun.

CONCLUSION

Thanks for making it through to the end of this book. We hope it was informative and able to provide you with all of the tools you need to achieve your goals whatever they may be.

The next step is to apply everything that you have learned. It is time for you to open an account with a trustworthy broker and start trading. Feel free to review the pages in this book and ensure that you have mastery of the details. Once you are confident enough, then it is your time to turn the forex market into a goldmine.

Trading currencies can be a very lucrative career. It is not a secret that many professional traders consider this activity as their full-time profession. They were able to quit their 8-hour employment and now engage in forex trading as a living. This is also possible for you. However, you should understand that this is something that you cannot do without making sacrifices. You need to spend time and put a lot of effort into learning how to trade effectively. This would mean spending hours doing careful research and analysis. You should also develop and test your trading strategy countless times. As a professional trader, you are responsible for all your actions. Therefore, you need to be careful, especially when trading using real money.

Being a forex trader can be a very fun career. Of course, if you get really good at it, then you might even be able to make your way to financial freedom. Every day, many professional traders around the world are making a decent profit. If you think that you have what it takes to be a successful FX trader, then it is time for you to take positive actions and change your life.

FOREX TRADING

Proven Forex Trading Money Making Strategy - Just 30 Minutes A Day

© Copyright 2018 by Lee Digital Ltd - All rights reserved.

The follow eBook is reproduced below with the goal of providing information that is as accurate and reliable as possible. Regardless, purchasing this eBook can be seen as consent to the fact that both the publisher and the author of this book are in no way experts on the topics discussed within and that any recommendations or suggestions that are made herein are for entertainment purposes only. Professionals should be consulted as needed prior to undertaking any of the action endorsed herein.

This declaration is deemed fair and valid by both the American Bar Association and the Committee of Publishers Association and is legally binding throughout the United States.

Furthermore, the transmission, duplication or reproduction of any of the following work including specific information will be considered an illegal act irrespective of if it is done electronically or in print. This extends to creating a secondary or tertiary copy of the work or a recorded copy and is only allowed with express written consent from the Publisher. All additional right reserved.

The information in the following pages is broadly considered to be a truthful and accurate account of facts and as such any inattention, use or misuse of the information in question by the reader will render any resulting actions solely under their purview. There are no scenarios in which the publisher or the original author of this work can be in any fashion deemed liable for any hardship or damages that may befall them after undertaking information described herein.

Additionally, the information in the following pages is intended only for informational purposes and should thus be thought of as universal. As befitting its nature, it is presented without assurance regarding its prolonged validity or interim quality. Trademarks that are mentioned are done without written consent and can in no way be considered an endorsement from the trademark holder.

INTRODUCTION

Congratulations on downloading *Forex: Proven Forex Trading Money Making Strategy – Just 30 Minutes a Day* and thank you for doing so. When it comes to pure money-making potential in the traditional investment markets, there are few better choices than investing in the forex market as only there will you find margin rates of 100:1 or more. For the unaware, this means that for every dollar you invest you have the opportunity to profit as if you invested $100. What's more, inside you will ultimately learn how to profit from trading in the forex market for just 30 minutes per day.

While you won't be able to find success trading for just 30 minutes per day right out of the gate, once you do your due diligence and learn the ropes of the market you will be able to cut down the day to day work you need to do substantially and the following chapters will teach you how to do just that. Trading in the forex market isn't without risks of its own, however, which is why you will also learn a wide variety of ways to ensure you maximize your gains while minimizing your losses at the same time.

In the following chapters, you will find tips on money management, cultivating a successful trading mindset, as well as how to analyze trades using both fundamental and technical analysis. You will also learn a variety of different trading strategies including several to help you get started and several more that you can tackle when you feel ready to get more advanced. Finally, you will find a wide range of tips designed to ensure you can cut down on your overall trading time as quickly as possible.

There are plenty of books on this subject on the market, thanks again for choosing this one! Every effort was made to ensure it is full of as much useful information as possible, please enjoy!

CHAPTER 1: FOREX TRADING BASICS

When it comes to the daily trading amount for the various investment markets, the foreign exchange market, more commonly known as the forex market, blows everything else out of the water. Every day it averages roughly four trillion dollars which dwarfs what the New York Stock Exchange is able to put out by more than 1,000 percent. Despite the potential for profit from so much money changing hands, private traders have only been able to take start taking advantage of this market relatively recently as prior to this point the technological requirements of forex trading limited this avenue to professional trading firms.

These days, there are a wide variety of different online forex trading platforms which means that the opportunity to profit from this massive market is open to anyone who is willing to put the time in to do it properly. However, before you get started, it is important to understand that the forex market is purely speculative which means that, unlike many other types of investing, all that is being exchanged in the average transaction is lines on various online ledgers. In fact, the entire forex market is purely limited to numbers in various computer databases with relevant information relating to the countries in question causing them to either move in one direction or another. As such, every transaction that is made is then tracked with any potential gains or loses expressed in the primary currency of your choice.

If this seems like an odd way to go about this entire process, that's because it wasn't designed with traders like you in mind. Instead, the forex market was created so that countries and international corporations could easily convert large amounts of money into various currencies without going through more traditional, and complicated, means. When these entities make these sorts of trades, the deal in amounts that are large enough to affect the overall valuation of one or both of the currencies in question.

On an average day, only about 20 percent of the forex market's activity comes from these market defining forces, with the rest coming from investors at varying levels who are interested in making money based on the way various currencies are moving at the moment. Of that 80 percent, about 50 percent are traders from financial institutions or hedge funds, though more and more private traders are getting in on the fun on a regular basis.

Forex basics

The most important thing to understand when it comes to forex trading is that forex trades always trade a pair of currencies instead of a single asset such as with most common stock market or options trade. To break this down even further, that means that with every trade, an options trader is always purchasing one currency while selling another. Furthermore, currency is primarily traded in 3 different quantities, often referred to as lots. A micro lot is 1,000 units of a given currency while a mini lot is 10,000 units of a currency and a standard lot is 100,000 units of a specific currency.

Additionally, you will want to remember that the smallest amount that a currency can move at a time is one percent of its total. This amount is known as a pip. Early on you are going to want to stick to trading in micro lots as this means a pip is only going to be worth about 10 cents. This will provide you with a buffer during the difficult early days when you will likely find the market turning against you in unexpected ways. Once you build up your confidence somewhat, you will be able to move up to the mini lot where a pip is worth $10. When it comes to determining your personal level of acceptable risk, you will want to always keep in mind that around 100 pips of movement is considered average for most trading sessions.

While the forex market has a few things about it that makes it different than other markets, it is still the same as other investment markets in the ways that matter most. Specifically, this means it is still driven by the rules of supply and demand at its heart. This means, that when a given currency is extremely high in demand, then its value will increase to compensate. This will continue until the supply exceeds the demand, at which point the price will drop to a point that allows it to once again be attractive to investors.

As a forex trader, you are going to want to be aware of when a particular currency is going to increase in demand so that you can get in on it on the ground floor. This means you are always going to want to be aware of important interest rate movements, geopolitical strife and economic predictions related to various world powers. When planning out the research you are going to do, it is important to also keep in mind that the forex market never actually closes from Monday to Friday so there is always something new to learn, regardless of the time of day it is. Rather, it is closed from

Friday night to Monday morning and specific currency pairs are typically only traded in an eight-hour window where those in its region are most active. There are three main sections to the forex trading day, US, Asia and Europe.

While there is no hard and fast rule saying the market needs to be split up in this way, it is a natural effect of the fact that currencies are always going to be worth more when that part of the world is the most active. For example, if you are interested trading in pairs based around the United States and various Asian markets then you would find those prices to be higher during the US portion of the day and again when the market starts moving in Asia in a big way.

While there are currency pairs for practically any two currencies imaginable, there are 18 major currency pairs that are going to be traded the most a majority of the time. These 18 pairs are, in turn, made up of just 8 currencies that you are going to need to be familiar with if you hope to find success in the forex market. These are AUD the Australian dollar, CAD the Canadian dollar, CHF the Swiss franc, EUR the euro, GBP the British pound, JPY the Japanese yen, NZD the New Zealand dollar and USD the US dollar.

While you may want to branch out into the occasional non-popular currency pair, starting with these early on will give you a focal point early on to limit what you need to learn before you can get started. It is important to take things slow and start with only one or two currency pairs early on for the best results.

Regulation

Another significant difference when it comes to the forex market that you will want to be aware of is that it operates without any type of regulatory body. Essentially, what this means is that if someone makes a trade in bad faith then there isn't anyone around to stop them directly. This also means there are no guarantees, no clearing houses and no arbitration. Instead, everyone trading in the forex market simply operates in good faith, knowing that if they want to keep making money from the market they are going to have to continue playing by the rules.

While this might seem like too big of a risk to take, the truth of the matter is that this level of regulation is actually quite effective as there is no alternative for those who find themselves blacklisted for bad behavior. Additionally, there is a voluntary organization, National Futures Association that holds its members to a higher standard when it comes to both fair conduct and arbitration. This means that when you are dealing with a Forex broker or dealer in the US then you are going to want to make sure they are NFA members to ensure you start off from as safe of a position as possible.

As there is no regulatory body to pick up the slack, the forex market also more relaxed rules than you might expect in a few other areas as well. For starters, you aren't limited when it comes to the number of short sells you can complete in any period of time. As such, if you find out that a given currency pair is about to take a colossal nosedive, then you can short it for as long as it is profitable to do so. In the previous sentence, you may have noticed the lack of the word research, this is because you don't have to worry about where you get your information when it comes to the forex market, everything is fair game. Furthermore, there are no limits to the size of individual trades which means you could do 100 lots if you could find a way to finance the trade.

You will also want to keep in mind that you won't find many traditional forex brokers around, as the forex market is principal only which means the role of broker is filled by what are known as dealers instead. Dealers directly take on any risk that may be associated with a given currency pair as they buy and sell directly from their personal stock making money on the disparities available to them just like anyone else.

As such, it is impossible to buy on the bid or sell at the offer when trading in forex; but this limitation is mitigated somewhat by the fact that it is much easier to make a profit from a forex trade because you do not need to worry about fees or commissions muddying the waters of the point that things swing in your favor and you start to make a profit.

Making a forex trade

As already noted, currency trades are always made in pairs which means you will be (ideally) selling one for a profit while you buy the second on the cheap. The currency being sold is known as the short position and the one being purchased is known as the long position. For example, if you decide to make a trade of EUR/USD then you are going long on dollars while going short on euros which means you are selling euros and buying dollars.

As previously mentioned there are only a set number of currencies that you need to focus on while you are a beginner to get a better idea of what the world of forex trading looks like. With that knowledge in hand then you are likely going to want to start with the following frequently traded pairs

- EUR/USD
- USD/JPY

- GDP/USD

- USD/CHF

Besides these extremely popular pairs, there are 3 other pairs that are known as the commodity pairs because the countries that they are comprised of move commodities around in very large amounts. The commodity pairs are:

¥ AUD/USD

¥ USD/CAD

¥ NZD/USD

Finally, 7 pairs, in addition to those 3 pairs listed below account for more than 90 percent of all of the trades that are made every day. The remaining 3 pairs include:

¥ EUR/JPY

¥ GBP/JPY

¥ EUR/GDP

Quoting a currency: When written, the currencies in your specific forex trades are always quoted in the same fashion. The first is what is known as the base currency and the second is known as the counter currency. In most instances, you will find that USD is generally assumed to be the base currency of the forex market as a whole with gains being written out in dollars per the primary currency and will be included as both the bid and ask price.

The bid price is the amount that a dealer will be willing to purchase the base currency at and it will generally be expressed in terms of the amount of the second currency. Meanwhile, the ask price is going to be the amount the dealer can expect to sell a unit of base currency for, and this is what is expressed in the counter currency. The difference between the two is known as the spread and it is in this space that dealers make a profit. Spreads are typically written out to the fourth decimal place.

Understanding margin: When it comes to trading in the forex market successfully, you will need to be aware that margin works differently here than it does elsewhere. Specifically, when it comes to forex, your margin should no longer be considered a down payment on equity that is going to materialize in the future. Rather, it can be considered an account deposit that can be used to help mitigate losses related to forex trades that may materialize down the line. As a general rule, the more leverage that a deal or even a broker allows, the high the margin on that trade is likely to be.

Additionally, in the forex market return and yield are connected directly which means that each time you complete a forex trade the currency you sell is paying for the currency you buy. You will still need to account for interest on the currencies you sell while seeing a bonus on the currencies you purchase.

Rollover: You will also need to be aware of the fact that all forex trades are mutually agreed upon to be completed in just two days. This period can be extended through what is known as a rollover which will give you an extra two days, as long as you are willing to pay extra for the interest on the transaction. There is no limit to the number of times you can invoke a rollover, though you will want to keep track of the fees as are sure to add up quickly.

When it comes to a rollover transaction, the difference between the two currencies you are working with is often visualized as what is known as an overnight loan. With an overnight loan, a trader retains a long position under the assumption that the interest rate will move in a positive way overnight. The amount gained from holding it through a rollover will vary daily based on the change in interest rates both experience. Avoiding a rollover is easy as well if you decide to go that route. All you need to do is ensure that you close out any of your positions when you close out for the evening.

Leverage: When dealing with the forex market leverage is the money that is borrowed with the intent of generating significantly increased returns for a given trade. While the amount of available leverage is often restricted in investment markets, rates of greater than 100 to 1 are available in the forex market which means that, if you choose a successful trade you can see the benefits of trading a lot for the price of trading a micro lot. Of course, leverage is not without its own type of risk as if you make a poor trade you will then be on the hook for a lot's worth of debt in addition to the micro lot that you just lost. Needless to say, it is best to stay away from trading with leverage until you are far more familiar with the ins and outs of the forex market.

Forex currency lingo

Cable, sterling, pound: These are the various names that you will see the UK's currency referenced as.

Greenback, buck: These are the most common slang terms for the US dollar in forex circles.

Swissie: You will often see the Swiss franc referred to as a Swissie in forex media.

Aussie: You will often see the Australian dollar referred to as the Aussie in forex publications.

Kiwi: You will often see the New Zealand dollar referred to as the Kiwi in forex publications.

Loonie, Little Dollar: You will often see the Canadian dollar referred to as the Little Dollar or sometimes the Loonie in forex publications.

Yard: A billion units of a specific currency is referred to as a yard.

CHAPTER 2: PROPER MONEY MANAGEMENT

If you believe the hype that many get rich quick trading scheme's promise, then finding the right trading strategy is akin to a silver bullet, the one answer to your prayers that will ensure that you can start making money hand over fist, without fail, 100 percent of the time. Unfortunately, the truth is much less enticing and requires far more hard work, starting with an understanding of proper money management techniques that will ensure that when you do start turning a profit it doesn't slip through your fingers before you've had time to enjoy it. Especially if you plan on working with leverage in the future, money management is a skill you should work on before you put a single cent into the market.

Understand the way of things: One of the most important things you need to do, right from the start, in order to ensure your forex trading career is both long and fruitful is to have a realistic understanding of just what it is you are getting yourself into. Specifically, that while leverage can be used to effectively generate gigantic windfalls in short periods of time, this is always going to be the exception, never the rule. As such, 99 times out of 100, if you make a move on an especially risky leveraged endeavor the only thing you are going to do is find yourself in a very expensive hole you have no way of climbing back out of.

What this means is that the most effective way to ensure your profits are only going to increase is to ground your expectations early on and never let them wander. While it might be difficult to keep your impulses in check, at first, eventually you will find that taking a realistic approach will help to ensure that you don't feel the need to reach for leverage beyond your station in the first place.

While trading in this fashion might cause you to see big returns temporarily, you are likely to lose it all just as quickly, resulting in little to no net gain. The most important thing you can do as a new trader is accept how much you currently have in your trading account and not try to artificially inflate that number. Remember, slow and steady wins the race.

Only trade what you can afford to lose: A core tenant of trading in the securities markets is that no trade, no matter how good it looks on paper, is ever going to be a sure thing. As such, if you hope to be able to trade effectively then you need to ensure that you are only ever trading with money that you can afford to lose. If you make the mistake of attempting to trade with money that you have a more immediate use for, then you are likely to have a skewed focus during the trade, which is far more likely to see you lose it all because you were unable to pull the trigger when the time was right.

This situation is obviously untenable as you need to be comfortable walking away from the money you have invested so far as a means of preventing greater losses in the long-term. When trading, your goal should be to remain as robotic as possible, any time you let your emotions start dictating your actions is a moment when you are putting your trading capital at risk. If you are trading with money that makes it difficult for you to make the hard calls in the moment, then you aren't going to maximizing your trades to their full potential, it is as simple as that.

This means you will likely need to have a conversation with yourself when-in you decide how much money you would be comfortable losing, not just in the short-term, but as if it caught on fire and disappeared completely. Whatever this amount is, this is the amount that you should put into a given trade, at least until you have improved your skills to the point that you are less concerned with the potential for a misstep.

Consider your thoughts on risk: While there is no simple way to determine the right amount of risk for you, it is still a decision you are going to need to make for yourself in order to make it in the forex trading world successfully. Some people are going to be able to sleep soundly at night after making risky trades and others are going to end up being awake all night when any trade is left on the table. There is nothing inherently wrong with either of those positions, as long as you determine which side of the coin you fall on before you start making trades. Taking trades that are outside of your comfort level, even if someone you trust says it's a good idea, will only lead to trouble in the long run as you will essentially be trying to jam a square peg into a round hole.

After you have gone ahead and determined the best amount of trading risk to focus on for you, you will then be able to focus your trading strategies around those that naturally align with the level of risk you are willing to take on in a given scenario. Using strategies that line up with your thoughts will allow what you are doing to work in tandem, which will ultimately allow you to trade more confidently than would otherwise be the case.

Once you have a clear understanding on the level of risk you prefer, along with the strategies that emphasize it, you will them be able to more easily determine how often you are going to need to trade in order to make the amount of money you are hoping for while trading in the forex market. Generally speaking, the greater your tolerance for risk, the more trades you will need to make in order for you to hit your target, though the overall profit is likely going to be higher when you do hit on a successful trade. As such, when it comes to determining your overall tolerance for risk, you will also need to consider how comfortable you are micromanaging trades versus setting them up and letting them run themselves.

Compartmentalize your trades: Another part of managing your forex trading capital successfully is learning to compartmentalize each trade which means not letting any individual loss, or win, influence the way you approach your next trade. Regardless of your intentions, doing so will make it much easier to fall victim to emotional trading, which is a surefire way to kiss your potential profits goodbye. This means you are going to want to do your best not to become over-confident but also avoid making revenge trades as both are likely to lead to the same outcome in the long run and it won't be good.

If you find yourself losing your objectivity, then it may be best to stop trading for a little while to ensure that you can calm down and remove yourself from the previous situation. If your previous trades are hanging over your head, then you are going to be splitting your focus instead of putting it all where it needs to be which is on the trade that you are about to make so you can ensure that you are managing your money properly.

If you find yourself losing your objectivity, then it may be best to stop trading for a little while to ensure that you can calm down and remove yourself from the previous situation. If your previous trades are hanging over your head, then you are going to be splitting your focus instead of putting it all where it needs to be which is on the trade that you are about to make so you can do everything in your power to ensure that each and every trade is appropriately successful.

Never take your trades personally: May new forex traders make the mistake of personifying specific trades they hold on to for purely emotional reasons. This is only going to cause you trouble in both the short and the long-term, however, as all of your trades should be based on cold hard facts and nothing else. If you start making trades based on anything else, the only thing you can expect to do is to start mismanaging your trading accounts in a big way. Furthermore, it is important to keep in mind that the market doesn't care about your hopes and dreams, it is simply a force that responds to what the traders demand.

Furthermore, you are going to want to avoid growing overconfident if you make several successful trades in a row, just as you will want to avoid losing your confidence if you have a bad trading day, or three, in a row. While it can be hard to believe, even the best traders in the world have off weeks, just as they have hot streaks that make up for the difference. Remaining neutral in your approach to trading is the only way to guarantee that your emotions don't skew the number and cause you more losses than you might otherwise experience.

Patience is a virtue: When it comes to managing your money effectively in the forex market, patience can be directly equated to long-term success. While you may initially feel the urge to trade constantly, it is important to understand that there are always going to be periods where the best way to ensure your profits to avoid trading at all. The market moves in a variety of ways and relatively few of them are going to result in the types of strong trends that you are looking for.

If you are convinced that you need to make trades every single day, consider the fact that the average across all types of investments is only 7 percent per year. Even if you aren't trading constantly, then you can realistically expect between 5 and 10 percent per month when starting out which still means you are going to be well ahead of the game. Instead of worrying about not trading enough, focus on making the most out of every trade that you do make, and you will see better results in the long-term practically guaranteed.

CHAPTER 3: CULTIVATE A FOREX MINDSET

When you are first starting out, it can be easy to feel as though the market itself, or perhaps the system that you are using, that is holding you back. Unfortunately, the truth of the matter is that there are other people who are in your same situation that are finding success, so there must be something more to it. That special sauce is a proper forex trading mindset and it is what separates successful forex traders from those who give up after the first six months.

The way you are wired

A successful trading mindset is actually a combination of three equally important things, the way your brain is wired, your mindset and psychological conditioning.

The way the brain works is that neurons fire in reaction to external stimuli and then travel along the easiest path possible to get where they are going. The more commonly used a path is, the more likely it is going to be used in the future.

These pathways then lead to habits and thoughts that form the basis for the things you do most frequently. When you put your pants on, do you always lead with your right foot? This is because the neural pathway that says this is the way things should be is much more worn in than the path that would see you lead with your left foot.

Furthermore, when the same group of neurons fires at the same time on a regular basis, the brain starts associating their various stimuli together as well. The end result of this is that thoughts that are unrelated on the surface can actually have major effects on the way your mind approaches the idea of trading. Generally speaking, the brain has three main functions, the first of which is regulation which handles all of the core physiological processes that keep you alive and kicking. The next is learning, which takes care of things like building new neural pathways and forming mental circuits. Finally, selection works with the other two to determine if the experience you are currently living through is worth storing away as experience for later. All three are crucial when it comes to trading successfully in the forex market.

Regulation: Understanding how to keep your breathing in line as a means of relaxation is crucial to your long-term success as a forex trader. Learning to breathe slowly and deeply, and essentially forcing yourself to relax, will help to prevent you from feeling emotional, panicked or stressed when trading, improving your overall successful trade percentage in the process. Failing to do so means you are going to be more likely to miss crucial details or make decisions that you would not make if you were in your right mind. Luckily, this is an easy skill to improve upon and you can do so by practicing yoga or mindfulness meditation.

Learning: The easiest ways to accelerate the learning process is to spend more time considering the feedback the market gives you, practicing your system or training with a mentor. Once you get into the habit of making learning a lifelong goal, you will find that you naturally improve as a forex trainer.

Selection: In addition to learning, taking more time to experience what the market has to offer will provide you with additional feedback and context that will help you naturally learn what strategies and practices are naturally more valuable and beneficial to your personal trading style. This will occur naturally as you discover what practices tend to make your money more consistently compared to those that do not.

Hardwired for survival: While modern society means you have had to learn countless bits of information that would be completely useless out of context, you have also picked up a wide variety of survival strategies along the way, likely many more than you might expect. These may not all be well-adapted for use in everyday life, however, which is why it is important to learn about why you think about certain things in the way you do.

For example, when the brain takes note of a high energy signal it typically triggers an alarm response which naturally triggers a host of nonproductive ways. Survival strategies to be aware of include:

• Prioritizing stability during periods of constant change

• Creating cause and effects relationships

• Attempting to avoid pain while seeking out pleasure

Depending on your trading style, prioritizing stability can either be a useful tool or one you will want to work to change. If you have a low tolerance for risk, then you will want to go with the flow and seek out stable trades when the market is in flux. However, if you prefer higher risks and greater rewards then you will want to be aware of this instinct so that you can more easily ignore it.

When it comes to being on the lookout for cause and effect scenarios, it is important to always keep in mind that the human mind is naturally fond of patterns which means that it likes to find them even in places where they might not actually be. As such, when you come across what you believe to be a relationship it is important to take a closer look and ensure that it really exists before acting on it in a way that you may regret later.

If you find yourself seeking to avoid pain and seek out pleasure, you are going to want to do what you can to change this mindset as soon as possible. Risk and reward are intertwined to the point where you cannot get one without the other. If you brain associates risk with pain, then you are going to need to do whatever it takes to change that mindset ASAP. Regardless, understanding why you may feel uneasy about a given trade, even after doing the necessary research will make it easier for you to push forward, eventually rewiring your neural pathways in the process.

Maximize your beliefs

Take a closer look at your beliefs

As a new trader, the sheer potential awaiting you in the forex market must make the possibilities seem endless. However, after you hit your first serious obstacle, whether that's a serious loss, misreading the market in a major way or any one of dozens of common new trader issues, you may find that your enthusiasm for the process overall may weaken. This, in turn, can make it even more difficult to trade successfully while at the same time dragging the goals you have set for yourself even further out of reach. If left unchecked, this can be the start of a pattern that can make it difficult, if not impossible, to be as successful as you would like.

These types of thoughts are known as limiting beliefs and they can manifest in a wide variety of unproductive trading habits. These include things like forcing yourself to overextend in an effort to double up after a previous loss, using more leverage than is prudent, variating from your trading plan without a good reason for doing so or doubting yourself when it comes to making a completely viable trade. Likewise, if you find yourself hesitating when it comes to determining a viable entry or exit point or making excuses for trades that ended up not working out in your favor, including blaming the market, then you might be dealing with limiting beliefs.

These beliefs may have already been a part of your subconscious, or they may have been created as you learned the wrong lessons from early trading experiences. The source of these issues isn't nearly as important as the fact that they are limiting your ability to trade successfully, and they need to be culled from your trading habits if you hope to turn a profit in the long-term. Whether you are aware of the fact or not, the market is essentially a mirror that affects what is in your mind. It doesn't have any actual biases, it simply reflects back your beliefs about yourself and your trading skill.

As such, when you engage in limiting beliefs, you are letting them deceive you and costing yourself money in the process. On the contrary, engaging in healthy, energetic, vibrant and clear energies will allow you to focus on the best your mind has to offer, improving the percentage of your successful trades as a result.

Moving beyond your limiting beliefs: The two most important traits you need to strengthen your mindset and banish your limiting beliefs are awareness and recognition. To start, you are going to want to make every effort to build up your awareness in such a way that it can be applied directly to your trading experiences. Doing so will allow you to see the way in which your limiting beliefs are directly tied to your successful trade percentage. It is this level of recognition that is required before you can realize not only that you have been unsuccessful but why exactly it is that success is eluding you.

You may find it useful to think of trading in the same way you would riding a horse. Specifically, it is bumpy and can often leave you feeling as though you are not in control. However, if you do your best to stay in the saddle, then eventually you will have enough knowledge to apply what you have learned so that you can progress on your way to success. Applying concentration and awareness to your daily training routine will help you build up mental strength and confidence as you see it lead to greater and greater success. This, in turn, will lead to an increase in trading skills from reading price action to being more disciplined.

Improve your posture: While not something you would likely expect to affect your mindset; the truth of the matter is that your physical posture can go a long way towards destroying any limiting thoughts that might be lying about. Specifically, you are going to want to ensure that you are sitting straight, with your spine properly aligned. This posture will improve not just your thought process but the way you breathe as well.

Keeping your spine straight will make it easier for your energy to move from your head directly to your heart, which will, in turn, allow you to think more clearly. If you sit with your neck bent at an odd angle, it limits the flow of this energy and isolates your head from this natural flow. If you often feel as though you are stuck in your head, this could very well be the reason why.

Improve your focus: In order to improve your focus during the trading day, you will want to start off with a round of mindfulness meditation to improve your ability to focus and make quick decisions in the moment. To begin, you simply try and remaining as fully in the current moment as possible by breathing slowly and taking the time to really listen to everything your senses are telling you. Start by slowly breathing in and out and focus on every second that this action requires.

From there, the biggest hurdle you will have to face is learning how to dismiss your thoughts without interacting with them. Mindfulness meditation is all about existing in the present as much as possible and listening to everything your senses have to tell you. In order for this to be the case, you must make a concentrated effort to keep your mind as clear as possible. No one's mind is ever truly free from other thoughts and ideas, however, which is why it is important for you to make every attempt to reduce excess thoughts as much as possible.

To do this, you must first make it a point to not feel angry or sadden at the fact that your mind is not completely clear, feeling something in relation to the thoughts is akin to interacting with them, the last thing you want to do. Instead, it may help to think of your mind as a blank space with bubbles floating through it. When a stray thought appears in a bubble, simply visualize it floating away and popping, removing the thought from your notice. Once mastered, this same technique can be used to ensure you maintain self-discipline and focus on the task at hand regardless of whatever it may be.

Become more aware of your positive thoughts: If you feel yourself starting to lend unreasonable credence to negative thoughts, you may instead find it useful to counter this influx of negative with an influx of positivity instead. Doing so will allow you to more clearly see the instances where your negative thoughts are trying to influence your actions, leading to a more stable trading experience as a result. With practice, this will also make it easier for you to improve your understanding of the market and improve your confidence as a result.

While the positive energy generated by this practice will likely start off as a slow trickle, if you nurture it you will find that it becomes a raging river before you know it. This will, in turn, make it easier for you to avoid engaging in excuses, negative emotions or anything else that is sure to have a negative effect on your ability to trade effectively.

CHAPTER 4: FUNDAMENTAL ANALYSIS

In order to trade in the forex market successfully, one of the most important things you can learn is the most reliable way to spot a trade that is going to end up being reliably profitable from one that blows up in your face. This is where proper analysis comes in handy, whether technical or fundamental. Fundamental analysis is easier to learn, though it is more time consuming to use properly, while technical analysis can be more difficult to wrap your mind around but can be done quite quickly once you get the hang of it. While both will help you to find the information you are looking for, they go about doing so in different ways; fundamental analysis concerns itself with looking at the big picture while technical analysis focuses on the price of a given currency in the moment to the exclusion of all else.

This divide when it comes to information means that fundamental analysis will always be useful when it coms to determining currencies that are currently undervalued based on current market forces. The information that is crucial to fundamental analysis is generated by external sources which means there won't always be new information available at all times. This chapter and the next are dedicated to fundamental and technical analysis, respectively.

Generally speaking, fundamental analysis allows you a likely glimpse at the future of the currency in question based on a variety of different variables such as publicized changes to the monetary policy that the countries you are interested in might affect. The idea here is that with enough information you can then find currency pairs that are currently undervalued because the market hasn't yet had the time to catch up with the changes that have been made. Fundamental analysis is always made up of the same set of steps which are described in detail below.

Start by determining the baseline: When it comes to considering the fundamental aspects of a pair of currencies, the first thing that you are going to want to do is to determine a baseline from which those currencies tend to return to time and again compared to the other commonly traded currency pairs. This will allow you to determine when it is time to make a move as you will be able to easily pinpoint changes to the pair that are important enough to warrant further consideration.

In order to accurately determine the baseline, the first thing you will need to do is to look into any relevant macroeconomic policies that are currently affecting your currency of choice. You will also want to look into the available historical data as past behavior is one of the best indicators of future evets. While this part of the process can certainly prove tedious, their important cannot be overstated.

After you have determined the historical precedent of the currency pair you are curious about, the next thing you will want to consider is the phase the currency is currently in and how likely it is going to remain in that phase for the foreseeable future. Every currency goes through phases on a regular basis as part of the natural market cycle.

The first phase is known as the boom phase which can be easily identified by its low volatility and high liquidity. The opposite of this phase is known as the bust phase wherein volatility is extremely high, and liquidity is extremely low. There are also pre and post versions of both phases that can be used to determine how much time the phase in question has before it is on its way out. Determining the right phase is a key part of knowing when you are on the right track regarding a particular trading pair.

In order to determine the current major or minor phase, the easiest thing to do is to start by checking the current rates of defaults along with banks loans as well as the accumulated reserve levels of the currencies in question. If numbers are relatively low them a boom phase is likely to be on its way, if not already in full swing. If the current numbers have already overstayed their welcome, then you can be fairly confident that a post-boom phase is likely to start at any time. Alternatively, if the numbers in question are higher than the baseline you have already established then you know that the currency in question is either due for a bust phase or is already experiencing it.

You can make money from either of the major phases as long as you are aware of them early on enough to turn a profit before things start to swing back in the opposite direction. Generally speaking, this means that the faster you can pinpoint what the next phase is going to be, the greater your dividends of any related trades will be.

Broaden your scope: After you have a general idea of the baseline for your favored currencies, as well as their current phases, the next thing you will need to do is look at the state of the global market as a whole to determine how it could possibly affect your trading pair. To ensure this part of the process is as effective as possible you are going to need to look beyond the obvious signs that everyone can see to find the indicators that you know will surely make waves as soon as they make it into the public consciousness.

One of the best places to start looking for this information is in the technology sector as emerging technologies can turn entire economies around in a relatively short period of time.

Technological indicators are often a great way to take advantage of a boom phase by getting in on the ground floor as, once it starts, it is likely to continue for as long as it takes for the technology to be fully integrated into the mainstream. Once it reaches the point of complete saturation then a bust phase is likely going to be on the horizon, and sooner rather than later. If you feel as though the countries responsible for the currencies in question are soon going to be in a post-boom or post-bust phase, then you are going to want to be very careful in any speculative market as the drop-off is sure to be coming and it is difficult to pinpoint exactly when.

If you know that a phase shift is coming, but you aren't quite sure when, then it is a good idea to focus on smaller leverage amounts than during other phases as they are more likely to pay off in the short-term. At the same time, you are also going to want to keep any eye out for long-term positions that are likely to pay out if a phase shift does occur. On the other hand, if the phase you are in currently is just starting out, you can make trades that have a higher potential for risk as the time concerns aren't going to be nearly serious enough to warrant the additional caution.

Look to global currency policy: While regional concerns are often going to be able to provide you with an insight into some long-reaching changes a given currency might experience in the near future, you are also going to want to broaden your search, even more, to include relevant global policies as well. While determining where you are going to start can be difficult at first, all you really need to do is to provide the same level of analysis that you used at the micro level on a macro basis instead. The best place to start with this sort of thing is going to be with the interest rates of the major players including the Federal Reserve, the European Central Bank, the Bank of Japan, the Bank of England and any other banks that may affect the currencies you are considering trading.

You will also need to consider any relevant legal mandates or policy biases that are currently in play to make sure that you aren't blindsided by these sorts of things when the times actually comes to stop doing research and actually make a move. While certainly time consuming, understanding every side of all the major issues will make it far easier to determine if certain currencies are flush with supply where the next emerging markets are likely to appear and what worldwide expectations are when it comes to future interest rate changes as well as market volatility.

Don't forget the past: Those who forget the past are doomed to repeat it and that goes double for forex traders. Once you have a solid grasp on the current events of the day, you are going to want to dig deeper and look for scenarios in the past that match what is currently going on today. This level of understanding will ultimately lead to a greater understanding of the current strength of your respective currencies while also giving you an opportunity to accurately determine the length of the current phase as well.

In order to ensure you are able to capitalize on your knowledge as effectively as possible, the ideal time to jump onto a new trade is going to be when one of the currency pairs is entering a post-boom phase while the other is entering the post-bust phase. This will ensure that the traditional credit channels are not exhausted completely, and you will thus have access to the maximum amount of allowable risk of any market state. This level of risk is going to start dropping as soon as the market conditions hit an ideal state and will continue until the situation with the currencies is reversed so getting in and making a profit when the time is right is crucial to your long-term success.

Don't forget volatility: Keeping the current level of volatility in mind is crucial when it comes to ensuring that the investments you are making are actually going to pay off in a reasonable period of time. Luckily, Luckily, it is relatively easy to determine the current level of volatility in a given market, all you need to do is to look to that country's stock market. The greater the level of stability the market in question is experiencing, the more confident those who are investing in it are going to remain when means the more stable the forex market is going to remain as well.

Additionally, it is important to keep in mind that, no matter what the current level of volatility may be, the market is never truly stable. As such, the best traders are those who prepare for the worst while at the same time hoping for the best. Generally speaking, the more robust a boom phase is, the lower the overall level of volatility is going to be.

Think outside the box on currency pairs: All of the information that you gather throughout the process should give you a decent idea regarding the current state of the currency pairs you are keeping tabs on. You should now have enough to be able to use this information to determine which pairs are going to be able to provide you with the most potential profit in not just the short-term but the long-term as well. Specifically, you are going to want to keep an eye out for pairs that have complimentary futures so that they will end up with the greatest gap between their two interest rates as possible.

Additionally, you are going to want to consider the gap between countries when it comes to overall output and unemployment rate. When looking into these differences you are also going to need to be aware of the fact that shortages can cause constraints to capacity or when the unemployment rate drops, both of which can lead to inflation as well. This, in turn, leads to an increase in interest rates which leads to a general cooling of the country's economy. As such, these factors are extremely important when it comes to determining the overall disparity between the interest rates of specific countries in the near future.

Furthermore, you are going to want to keep tabs on the amount of debt that the countries in question are dealing with, as well as their reputation of repayment on the global market. Specifically, you are going to want to look for a balanced capital to debt ratio as the healthier that this number is the stronger the national currency is going to be no matter what else is currently taking place. To determine this ratio, you will want to know how much capital each country currently has on hand as well as their position when it comes to other nations and their level of reserves and foreign investment.

Understand their relative trade strength: If you find a currency that is currently in the middle of a boom phase, the overall strength that its fundamentals show will determine how likely those who are holding it in various currency pairs are to hold or sell. The same also goes for currencies that boast an overly strong or overly weak interest rate when compared to other, similar currencies. What this means is that when a given currency is in the earliest part of the boom phase you will be able to easily find a strong market for its related currency pairs which combine agreeable fundamentals and strong interest rates. While all of these factors are important, as a general rule a strong interest rate will always trump subpar fundamentals.

Watch out for market sentiment

While determining specifics in undervalued currencies is useful most of the time, sometimes the market simply doesn't behave in the way that it realistically should. In these cases, it is the market sentiment that has hijacked the price of the currency in question and learning how to stay on the lookout for its influence is guaranteed to save you from some seriously unprofitable trades in the long run.

Like many things in the forex market, this is easier said than done, however, which is why it is best to take the following suggestions related to reading market sentiment to heart if you ever hope to get a clear idea of how strong the momentum regarding a given currency truly is.

Choose the right trend: Each and every move that a currency makes is ultimately based on a trend that started building hours, if not days before. As such, if you spend time trading with either the 15 or 60-minute chart then you may find yourself accidentally moving forward based on part of a larger trend that is ultimately going to end up moving in the opposite direction. As such, in order to avoid such mistakes, you are going to want to start by identifying the trend in the daily chart and then working inward from there until you reach your target chart. This will allow you to more easily determine the breadth of a given chart and allow you to avoid trading based on anterior movement as well.

Find the right price movement: On the topic of price movement, depending on the pair you are trading in, you will likely come across profits that you might not otherwise bank by simply getting a feel for the way your favored currency pairs move on a regular basis. Getting a feel for price movement means understanding the speed at which the pair typically moves, in both directions, to ensure that you know the most effective time to strike.

When the movement is clearly headed in an upwards direction with a quickness, only to slowly descend after the fact, time and again, then you can expect other traders to be steadily buying into the pair without taking the time to do all the relevant research. This, in turn, means you can expect the overall sentiment of the market to be bullish which means you can respond appropriately.

Similar information can also be determined based on the way the market responds when new relevant information, both positive and negative, comes to light. As an example, if there was just a round of positive economic news out of the United Kingdom but the positive change in the GBP and USD pair doesn't seem all that enthusiastic, then you can safely determine that the market is moving in a bearish direction when it comes to GBP/USD.

Watch your indicators of volume: While there are a wide variety of different indicators that measure volume, there are no better means for doing so than the Commitment of Traders Report which is released each and every Friday. This report clearly outlines the net of all the trades made, both long and short, for the week, for both commercial and private traders. This is a great place to start if you aren't sure what currencies to favor as this will show where most of the interest was for the proceeding week.

As previously noted, it is best to always trade on the trend which means that if there are more net longs overall you are going to want to buy and if there are more net shorts overall then you are going to want to sell. When this is not the case is if the buy positions are already at extreme levels then you will want to sell or at least wait until things move in the other direction because there can be no more increase if everyone who is going to buy has already bought. Eventually, you will see a reversal in this case which means that if this is the case then you are better off trading in the medium term instead.

Look more closely at international trends: When you are first getting your start in the forex market you are likely going to be surprised at just how interconnected the world as a whole really is. While some of these connections are going to be obvious, other will certainly catch you off guard the first time you encounter them which means you will want to pay attention to the way news affects various currency pairs, even if you are not actually trading in them at the moment as you never know when that information might be useful again at a later date.

CHAPTER 5: TECHNICAL ANALYSIS

In order to ensure that your successful trade percentage only continues to increase as time goes on, you will likely eventually find it useful to branch out from using fundamental analysis exclusively to using technical analysis as well. While some traders consider the two types of analysis to be at odds with one another, the fact of the matter is that a balanced approach that uses each, when required, is always going to be the most effective in both the short and the long-term.

Technical analysis studies past market trends with the goal of accurately predicting those that are likely to occur again in the future. Technical analysis is ideal for those that like the idea of determining future performance by looking at previous prices, without having to dig through mountains of paperwork to find the details you are looking for. While the past will never be able to truly predict the future 100 percent of the time, technical analysis is useful when combined with a basic understanding of market mentality for generating predictions that are accurate within reason.

Price charts

A price chart is the primary tool of technical analysis. As the name implies, it charts the price of a given currency, on the x axis, as time passes, on the y axis. There are several different types of charts to choose from, but if you are just getting started with technical analysis then you will want to start with the line chart, the point and click chart, the candlestick chart and the bar chart.

Line charts: The most basic chart of them all is the line chart. It shows the closing price for the currency in question over a set period of time. The titular line is then formed one the day's grouping of closing prices has been determined and they are then connected with the purpose of determining a trend. While it doesn't include relevant details such as opening price or the results for the day overall, it will tell you if the day is positive or negative while also cutting out all of the noise that is so common in most other charts. As such, it can be an extremely enlightening place to start if you are looking at a new currency for the first time.

Bar chart: When compared to a line chart, a bar chart adds in the additional details related to a currency's movement throughout each day. The top and the bottom of the bar are going to represent the high and low for the day respectively and the closing price is denoted by a dash found on the right side of the bar. Meanwhile, the dash on the left side of the bar is going to show the starting price. Finally, if the overall value of the currency increased for the day then the bar will be black and if it decreased it will be either red or clear depending on your trading software.

Candlestick chart: A candlestick is similar to a bar chart in many ways, though it also provides additional relevant information that is more detailed overall. It includes the range for the day, expressed as a line, as with a bar graph, but when you view a candlestick chart you will also notice a wide bar near the vertical line which indicates the degree of difference the price experienced over a given period of time. If the price increases for the day, then the candlestick will not be shaded in and if the price decreased throughout the day then it will typically be shaded in red as well.

Point and figure chart: While the point and figure chart are used less frequently than some of the charts that have been previously discussed, the point and figure chart has been in constant use for more than 100 years and can still provide insight when used correctly. Specifically, this chart is used to determine how much a price is likely to move without taking timing or volume into account. This makes it a pure indicator of price, without any of the market noise that might otherwise be attached.

A point and figure chart can be easily picked out from the crowd as it is made up of Xs and Os rather than lines and points. The Xs will indicate points where positive trends occurred while the Os will indicate periods of downward movement. You will also notice numbers and letters listed along the bottom of the chart which corresponds to months as well as dates. This type of chart will also make it clear how much the price is going to have to move in order for an X to become an O or an O to become an X.

Range and trend

In order to ensure that you can properly profit from the use of technical analysis, it is crucial that you determine if it makes more sense for your trading style to focus on trading via trend or trading via range. While the two are both based on the price of the currency in question, they use that information quite differently in practice which means you are going to want to focus on either one or the other for the best results.

If you feel as though your personal trading style would benefit from making trades that mostly go with the flow, then you are going to be more interested in trading via trend as this will tell you what other traders are up to. Your goal in situations like this will be to determine which trends are most likely going to be the most robust in the near future, so you have the maximum amount of time to jump on them, reaping a lion's share of the profits in the process. If you are considering this type of trading, then you will want to stick with smaller trades as you can lose out if a trend fails to materialize in the expected way at the wrong time. Trading via trend is ideal for those who prefer high risk and the greater potential for reward it brings along with it.

Range trading, on the other hand, is better suited for those who are willing to forgo some amount of profit for more reliable returns. The range in question is going to be the price that a given currency is going to return to twice or more throughout the time you are holding it, allowing you to profit each time. The market is going to present you with different challenges every single day in the form of different trends and potential opportunities.

Regardless of this fact, the movement typically tends to operate in ways that seem completely random, though its true intentions can be found once you determine where to look. The opening range has been profitable for trading professionals for decades as a profitable way to start off with an idea of the market's mood to make any profits that are coming up even easier to obtain.

When you take advantage of the opening range for a starting point, you ill then be able to locate the truth of the current market to determine if the bulls or bears are going to be in charge at the moment. In order to get the most out of this practice, it is crucial that you understand the opening range for low and high levels as they are of critical importance when it comes to levels of resistance and support throughout the day.

Understanding these details will make it far easier for you to anticipate levels in the market that are more likely to reverse or increase the changes you are seeing. Looking at the trading day from this perspective is going to make it easier for you to make the right moves at the right time to allow you to determine when future movement is forthcoming, so you can be in the right place at the right time.

This doesn't mean you won't be able to act if you can't find the perfect entry point each and every time. All it means is that you will simply need to get in at a point where you will be in an ideal position for the next time the cycle repeats itself. You should also keep in mind that of the two strategies, range trading can take more resources to utilize properly which means you will want to have a substantial bankroll before you put it into effect.

Start off on the right foot

In order to use technical analysis effectively, you will need to understand that it functions around the idea that the price of a given currency is going to fluctuate in the future based on a number of identifiable patterns that can be seen in its past. As such, unlike with fundamental analysis where you might have trouble finding enough data to make a rational choice, with technical analysis you will have more data than you can ever hope to sort through. You will have plenty of tools to help you sort through all of this information, including things like trends, charts and indicators that will point you in the right direction.

While many of the technical analysis techniques might seem overly complicated at first, at their most basic they are all looking for different ways to determine trends that are going to form in the future along with the strength. Choosing the right trends at the right time is the first step to becoming a successful forex trader in the long-term.

Understand the market: Technical analysis is all about measuring the relative value of a particular trade or underlying asset by using available tools to find otherwise invisible patterns that, ideally, few other people have currently noticed. When it comes to using technical analysis properly you are going to always need to assume three things are true. First and foremost, the market ultimately discounts everything; second, trends will always be an adequate predictor of price and third, history is bound to repeat itself when given enough time to do so.

Technical analysis also believes that the price of a given underlying asset is ultimately the only metric that truly matters when it comes to understanding the current state of the market. This is the case because any and all other facets of the market have already been factored through to the price before it reached the point it is currently at which means that analyzing anything besides the price is, simply put, a waste of time.

Furthermore, technical analysis holds to the fact that the value of the underlying asset in question moves based on a trend that is well established which means it can be tracked as long as you know what it is that you are looking for. From there, it is really just a matter of time before the trend comes back around and you can take advantage of it once more. This is a viable strategy as it is more likely that an existing trend is going to reemerge than it is for a completely new trend to show up in its place.

After all, history is always going to repeat itself. This isn't just a saying, it is an unavoidable part of human nature, specifically, people like patterns. This means that if there is a pattern in a series of data, you can expect people to find it. Once it is found, you can then rest assured that they will do everything they can to take advantage of it. This will be the case each and every time the pattern is found which means that, if you find the pattern first, you can set yourself up to take advantage of it in the most effective way possible.

This is what allows many of the common technical patterns that are in use today to continue to be useful despite the fact that they have been in use for 100 years or more. This just goes to show that public opinion and action in relation to price changes is always going to be the same no matter what.

All about trend: Being aware of trend and how it can affect the ways you will analyze a specific trade is key to your long-term success through technical analysis. When on the lookout for trend, it can be any clear direction that the price of a given currency is taking that is clear enough to cut through all of the noise that naturally infects the market as a whole. Trends can be either strong enough to see from a mile away or weak enough to easily miss even if you are looking for them. Essentially it just means that just because a given trend isn't immediately visible then this doesn't mean it isn't there. Likewise, you are going to always want to ensure that the trend you think you are following is really there as it can be easy to misinterpret false data if you aren't careful.

The best way to ensure that the trend you are following is actually worth following is going to be to focus exclusively on the lows and highs and leave everything else out of the equation. This way you will be able to easily determine if the lows continue to increase (signaling an uptrend) or if the highs continue to decrease (signaling a reversal). You may also uncover a horizontal trend which shows that nothing much of anything is happening at the moment and you might be better off waiting to get into the market until something more well-defined comes along.

Tapping into a specific long-lasting trend can allow you to assume that the net time it comes back around it is likely to be even more pronounced. You will want to keep an eye on things until the trend starts to materialize, however, just in case. If you find yourself watching a short trend, then you will need to expand your focus and ensure you aren't looking at a smaller part of a larger trend by mistake. The easiest way to do so is to simply choose a longer timeframe and see what there is to see.

While this will naturally make things more cumbersome, it can also make it far easier to catch a mistake that you may not otherwise be aware that you are making. The opposite can be true as well, if you are having trouble catching the right shorter trend, then a narrow focus across a shorter timeline might be just what the doctor ordered.

Trend mapping: After you have picked out the trend you are interested in finding more about, the next thing you will need to do is create a trendline that will let you map out all of the details as you come across them. This can be accomplished by simply drawing a straight line through the data points to make the trend more visible. If the trend is positive, then you will want to connect the dots of the various lows that are being measured while if it is a negative trend you will want to connect the relevant highs.

This line is what is known as the resistance line and it represents the market's natural inclination to push back once prices hit a point that is either significantly above or significantly below the average. This doesn't indicate the likelihood of the next price movement, just its overall limits. Once you have created the initial line, you will then want to create an additional pair of lines, one for the support level and one for the resistance level.

The support line will connect all of the lows while the resistance lines will connect all of the highs. The resulting channel that you then create will likely be either positive or negative though neutral channels representing sideways movement are also possible. Regardless, the channel you create needs to continue for a long enough time to show where the price breaks away from the status quo. This moment is going to represent your ideal entry point that will give you the best chance see the greatest overall return on your investment.

CHAPTER 6: FOREX STRATEGY BASICS

Once you know what to look for in a good trade, the next thing you are going to want to master is the basic short-term and long-term strategies that are most commonly used in the forex market. While the advanced strategies discussed in later chapters certainly have their place as well, you will likely find yourself using these strategies far more often, simply because they are useful in so many different situations.

Carry trades

If you are interested in making long-term trades in the forex market, then you are going to ultimately become very familiar with the technique known as the carry trade. This strategy involves finding a currency pair that your analysis indicates should be profitable in the near future while also having the greatest amount of disparity between their two interest rates as possible. Typically, one of the currencies that you are going to want to use for this type of strategy is going to be either the Australian dollar, the New Zealand dollar or the Japanese yen. The New Zealand dollar and the Australian dollar are known to frequently have an interest rate of as high as 4.5 while the Japanese yen is known for getting as low as 0.1.

When used correctly, a carry trade is an excellent way to add value to your portfolio as they are guaranteed to generate profit every day, based largely on interest, for each day you hold onto them. When making carry trades it is important to keep in mind that payments for interest earned during the weekend won't be paid until Wednesday which makes Thursday the most profitable day of the week to close out carry trades. The carry trade is also an excellent choice for those who don't want to spend each and every minute of every day staring at a computer screen in hopes of seeing the type of movement that will generate a reasonable amount of profit.

While it has been a part of the forex trader's toolbox for decades, the carry trade gained widespread usage in the early 00s when the AUD/JPY pair spent several months with an interest rate differential that was greater than five percent. This, coupled with the fact that leverage in excess of 200:1 was widely available meant that new investors were gaining and losing millions of dollars each week in a scenario that is surprisingly similar to the rush to buy Bitcoin in the fall of 2017.

In order to get an initial idea as to what a given carry trade can net you, the first step is to figure out the difference between the interest rate of the long and short currencies. With that number in mind, you will then multiply it by the number of units that you have in your position that is connected to the interest rate you are interested in, making a special point to include leverage as well. With this number in hand, you will then simply divide by 365 to find the amount of interest that you will earn each day.

When it comes to starting a new carry trade, the best time to do so is when a central bank report is released that indicates an increase in interest rates is forthcoming. After this information is released, you will find that countless traders jump on the idea of the carry trade using the currency whose interest rate is on the rise and its companion currency with the greatest overall degree of difference. Once you understand how the market is going to react to this news, it then becomes a matter of jumping on before the rush in order to ensure that your own profits are maximized as well. Remember, the longer you wait, the greater the starting differential will be and the less you will learn by an additional widening of the gap.

Basket carry: If the indicators on a given currency pair are not as strong as you may typically prefer, then a traditional carry trade might be a bit too risky to commit to whole-heartedly. If you have some type of information that makes you want to still pursue this course of action, then you will want to use a basket carry trade instead.

To do so, you will want to purchase three different currency pairs rather than just the one you are the most interested in. Each of these pairs should have varying interest rate levels so that you are virtually guaranteed to see a profit regardless of the direction the market ultimately moves in. When using this strategy, you will generally see an average profit on one of the three pairs and a small profit on the second while letting the third expire after only losing out on the transaction fees.

A carry trade is a great way to steady return on your initial investment without having to worry about watching the related currency movement too closely. This does not mean that it is always going to be the right choice in every situation, however. For example, if a country that has historically had a high interest rate suddenly dropped it dramatically in an effort to bolster their economy then those who are using it to prop up a carry trade are going to be forced to rapidly offload it, reducing the disparity for that pair even more. The same issue can occur if the reported average annual yield drops tenuously or the variance inherent in the exchange rate increases. Finally, you will want to always be on the lookout to ensure that the central bank of either country doesn't do anything to forcibly alter the current currency trajectory.

Trading in the short-term

If you are more interested in shorter timeframes than what a carry trade can offer you, then the most important thing to remember is that you are going to want to prioritize trades that allow you to remain in control at all times, both when it comes to managing risk and sticking to the plan you come up with prior to starting. This will allow you to deal in charts that offer shorter time frames than many other forex investors. This doesn't mean that you will only want to stick to the short-term charts, however, as this will unnaturally curtail your profits in a way that will only lose you money in the long run.

To get started trading in the short term, the first thing that you will need to do is to find a pair of moving averages on the hourly chart. The trading platform that you use should have an option to automatically generate what you are looking for based on a predetermined time frame that you plug in. Once you have the indicators that you are looking for you will then be able to utilize them as a type of guidepost, allowing you to see how the market is moving in a time frame that will allow you to look before you act. If the resulting short moving average is less than the greater moving average, then you are going to want to lean heavily on a long position while if the opposite is true then you will need to lean on the short position in order to profit from the transaction.

Once you have found the trend that you are comfortable working with, the next is going to be to look more closely at the entries to match the direction of the trend you are looking into. Your main goal at this time should be to pick out the momentum that you have already seen on a longer chart as it is visualized on the shorter five or 15-minute charts. When taking advantage of this type of strategy, it is important to keep in mind that the timing is not always going to be in your favor when it comes to buying in. Instead, you are going to want to wait patiently for a profitable position to come along and the most reliable way to know when it arrives is to look for what is known as an exponential moving average.

When looking for this average you are going to want to keep an eye out for the trigger known as the eight-period exponential on the five-minute chart. Once this exponential starts moving in the direction of the overall trend, you will know that the strength of the trend and the speed at which it is acted upon are only going to increase. While this strategy may take a fair amount of micromanaging, it is well worth it for several reasons, starting with the fact that if you wait for the right trigger you know that other short-term traders are creating action based on the pair you are most interested in which means you can practically guarantee reliable profits for yourself if you jump in at a smart time.

This strategy is also a great choice when you are first getting started in forex trading, especially if your trading capital is rather limited. This is due to the fact that it allows savvy traders to move in on specific currency pairs early enough to get a great deal before the actual momentum picks up steam and the bullish price movement pushes the pair into prohibitively expensive territory.

This is also a useful strategy if you are looking to maximize the currencies you are looking to sell as it will provide you with the opportunity to know when a mass exodus on the currency in question is going to occur, allowing you to sell when the price is still high. It is still important to keep in mind that if a price sees a retracement in the short-term then the price is likely going to swing quickly but you will still wan tot double check what you are seeing to prevent a costly mistake.

To further maximize your profits using this strategy you are going to want to set your stop losses so that they are placed below the most recent high-water mark. That is, of course, unless you are currently heavily invested in a short position in which case you will want to set your stop losses in such a way that they are above the most recent low point of the currency to ensure that you don't suffer a loss if the trend losses strength earlier than you were expecting. This makes the short-term strategy extremely versatile as long as you are able to keep your emotions in check and set the right stops and stick with them as opposed to losing yourself in the moment in hopes of seeing things turn around.

This is not to say that working in the short-term is without risk, and the opposite is actually true in most cases. The short-term charts are far more likely to change with little to no notice than the long-term charts are, simply because any change that is noticed is going to be noticed first there. This means that if you hope to make money by using this strategy then you are going to want to do everything in your power to guarantee you are free to act with only a moment's notice. The best reaction in most situations is going to be waiting for the currency to return to a point of profitability before setting a new stop loss that is slightly in the money without getting greedy.

CHAPTER 7: BOLLINGER BAND BOUNCE TRADING STRATEGY

Generally speaking, it is always going to be easier to trade based on an existing trend than it is to trade when one or both of your currencies in a pair is either rangebound or moving horizontally. This can be so difficult for many traders that they simply refuse to trade when the market is in this state and simply sit out the market until they can track down a stronger trend to follow. This only causes them to lose out on potential profits in the long-term, however, as there are still plenty of ways to make money without a strong trend to follow.

The Bollinger Band Bounce strategy is one such option, as it was created based on the way the price typically behaves when the Bollinger bands detect a limit when it comes to the range of movement the price can see in the short-term. Essentially, what this means is that the Bollinger bands have more elasticity than they normally do. In this type of scenario, the price frequently approaches the outer band before meeting with resistance and snapping back towards the opposite band.

After you have noticed this type of behavior taking place, you can then make excellent use of it by simply trading based on the action of the price as it moves back and forth between the outer bands. While this is not an especially useful strategy if the market is moving vigorously in one directly or another, it is a great way to scalp in a market that really isn't doing much of anything.

Start off right: In order to make the most out of this strategy, you will want to start by determining that the price is actually range bound. To do so, all you need to do is to use Bollinger bands to ensure the price is staying put, specifically on the same side of the middle Bollinger band each time it returns to that point. Assuming the price continues to rebound in the same way, then you can expect the existing trend to continue until this is no longer the case.

Tweezer bottom candlestick

One of the strongest indicators that the market is ranging is when a tweezer bottom candlestick pattern emerges. If this happens at the same time as a Fibonacci retracement, resistance and support level or relevant pivot level, then you will know the signal is almost too strong to contain. If this is the case, then you will be able to make a profit from trading at this level rather than waiting for the confirmation of a ranging price based on the way it reacts to the opposite band as you normally would.

This pattern is also easy to spot as it is actually made up of two different, separate, forex candle patterns. The first candle, known as the setup candle, is either going to be notably bullish or bearish and will ideally occur at the tail end of a substantial price push down. This candle represents the last vestiges of the downwards price surge and also a failure back from the low price.

The second candle is known as the confirmation candle and is always going to be bullish. The confirmation candle will have a peak price or lower wick that will match quite closely, or even exactly, with that of the setup candle. The stronger the signal, the greater the length of the confirmation candle wick. This represents the amount of low point rejection that is taking place.

Fundamentals to keep in mind: The tweezer bottom candlestick pattern is going to most commonly occur at the end of a trend towards decreasing prices, regardless if this is part of a larger trend or simply a short overall retracement. If this takes place at the end of a long-running price decrease, then it likely indicates that the supply of sellers is just about to run dry.

This then naturally means that the market of buyers who are eager for opportunities is going to be primed for action and more likely to jump into the market as the levels of the currency pair in question appear quite cheap. If there is a bear and bull struggle taking place as well, keep in mind that it is likely the bulls will come out on top. After this happens, the price will often settle near the higher point on the confirmation candle as well as at a point that is above where it started.

The tweezer bottom is also more likely to occur during a positive trend that causes the price to retrace to that of a previous support level. This will also cause some downward movement in part due to buyers striving to make a profit while at the same time sellers who are slow to move into the market in part thanks to inflated prices and in part simply because it is easy to see the overall number of buyers drying up. This, in turn, often causes the price to decrease to a level when buyers will once again be interested. This, eventually, will cause the price to be pushed up once again.

Generally speaking, in order to maximize the value potential from this situation, you are going to want to purchase a buy stop at a point between two and five pips above the highest price the confirmation candle has reached so far. If you are extremely confident about the state of the market, you could also choose to place an order that is at market. Regardless of your choice, you are still going to want to place a stop that is anywhere between two and five pips below the bottom most point of the tweezer bottom candlestick.

As always, this advice is simply a general guide as the current level of market volatility is going to play a huge part in where you place your stops. If you are working with a longer timeframe then setting a stop that is up to 20 pips below or above the current price is a perfectly viable strategy. The greater the size of the bullish confirmation candle, the greater the likelihood that the price is going to increase. This is only true up to a point, however, as if it is too long then you might have a difficult time finding an adequate risk and reward ratio.

As an example, if you set a stop loss that is 50 pips below the tweezer bottom just to manage the trade correctly and you know that there is resistance at 20 pips above the current price action then you can consider the trade to have a low possibility of success and pass on it.

Engulfing candlestick

In order to confirm the signals that you find in the bouncing Bollinger band strategy, you will want to be on the lookout for either bearish or bullish engulfing candlestick patterns. You can also look for an evening star. This type of candlestick pattern is made up of a pair of forex candles, both the confirmation and the signal are going to be contained within the second candle which is known as the confirmation candle. You will be able to recognize it due to its large body that completely consumes the setup candle. At close, the confirmation candle will have a lower overall price than the setup candle.

This type of pattern often starts near the top before continuing upward regardless of whether that move is connected to a retracement or a longer trend. If it appears at the end of the protracted price increase, then this is a signal that the supply of buyers is filling out the seller's market. Assuming this occurs, more sellers than ever are likely to jump on the bandwagon thanks to the high price of the currency pair. With one focused move, they then defeat the buyers by exceeding the bullish effort found in previous candles and reversing the price in the process.

You can also find a similar pattern in a downward trend assuming the price temporarily retraces to a predetermined resistance level. This typically occurs when a variety of different sellers all take their profits at once and buyers move in to rapidly take advantage of the deflating pricing. This can also occur as part of a normal period of market exhaustion. This, in turn, causes the price to move upward to a level where sellers can once again be reasonably interested in the currency and start pushing the price in a downward direction once more.

Bullish engulfing pattern: The bullish engulfing pattern is also made up of two separate candles, with both the confirmation and signal found within the second candle. In this pattern, the setup candle is bearish and typically occurs after a hard-downward price push. The second candle is also going to be bullish and contains a body that essentially engulfs the setup candle. The closing price of this candle is also greater than the setup candle.

The bullish engulfing pattern tends to set itself up at the bottom point of a downward price trend and typically signals that sellers are in low supply and the market is starting to favor buyers. This will attract new buyers who like the cheap price. In a concentrated push, they then overpower the sellers and exceed the bearish leaning, reversing the direction of the price.

Assuming this scenario forms during an uptrend, the price will naturally retrace itself to a support point and the downward move will cause additional sellers to take advantage of the high prices. This, in turn, will also cause the price to gently move in that same downward direction until the buyers are once again willing to bite. When this occurs, the price will move upward once more.

Limits and the bouncing Bollinger strategy

Once you have a clear idea of the type of indicators you are going to be on the lookout for, the next thing you are going to want to do is to take into account the mechanics surrounding this strategy's stop loss, entry, and take profit limits. When considering these limits, it is important to remember that this is a scalping strategy which means that your goal should be to enter immediately once the signal can be positively confirmed. Additionally, you will want to use a tight, aggressive stop loss and also a take profit limit that is set to the opposite of the mid-Bollinger band.

Once the move has been confirmed successfully, the next step is to move the stop loss to the breakeven point immediately to prevent an additional loss. If you miss this part of the process then you can find yourself losing out on profit if the price bounces off the middle band and then retraces before you can clear a profit, taking out your stop as it goes. This can happen in the first part of the trade as well, assuming you don't immediately move the breakeven point as soon as it is safe to do so.

There is no ideal time limit when it comes to moving the breakeven point and learning when to do so in order to maximize your profits will only come with practice. If you move to quickly then you will likely find that you are stopped via the expected retracement, even if the price is still actively moving in your direction when you initially move it. You will need to remain vigilant so that you don't miss your chance, without making the mistake of rushing either.

Generally speaking, this strategy is best used when the market is experiencing a lull which means no news announcement or the like are expected anytime soon. Furthermore, you are going to want to avoid using it on pairs that are prone to spiky price action. Finally, you are going to want to ensure that you aren't committing to this strategy just because the price reaches the outer band, additional verification is going to be required to ensure that this is the right move.

CHAPTER 8: FIBONACCI TRADING STRATEGY

Fibonacci numbers start with 0 and 1 and then increase exponentially from there by adding the 2 previous numbers together to get the next number in the sequence. As such it starts off with 0, 1, 2, 3, 5 and so on and so forth. The difference between these numbers is known as the Fibonacci ratio which includes .236, .382, .5 and so on and so forth. Finding these ratios in the pairs you are considering allows you to determine naturally occurring entry and exit points.

Using the Fibonacci sequence to perform a retracement gives you the ability to determine how much an asset moved in price initially. It uses multiple horizontal lines to point out resistance or support at either 23.6, 38.2, 50, 61.8 or 100 percent. When used properly they make it easier to identify the spots transactions should be started, what prices to target and what stop losses to set.

This doesn't mean that you should apply the Fibonacci retracements blindly as doing so can lead to failure as easily as it can success. It is important to avoid choosing inconsistent reference points which can easily lead to mistakes as well as misanalysis, for example, mistaking the wick for the body of a candle. Retracements using the Fibonacci sequence should always be applied wick-to-wick which in turn leads to a clearly defined and actionable resistance level.

Likewise, it is important to always keep the big picture in mind and keep an eye on trends that are of the longer variety as well. Failing to keep the broad perspective in mind makes short-term trades more likely to fail as it makes it harder to project the correct momentum and direction any potential opportunities might be moving in. Keeping the larger trends in mind will help you pick more reliable trades while also preventing you from accidentally trading against a specific trend.

Don't forget, Fibonacci retracements are likely to indicate quality trades, but they will never be able to do so in a complete vacuum. It is best to start with a retracement and then apply other tools including stochastic oscillators or MACD. Moving ahead without confirmation will leave you with little except positive thoughts and wishes that the outcome goes the way you want. Remember, there is no one indicator that is strong enough to warrant moving forward on a trade without double checking the validity of the data.

The other limitation of a Fibonacci retracement is that it doesn't work reliably over shorter time frames as there is simply too much interference from standard market volatility which will result in false apparent levels of support as well as resistance. What's more, the addition of whipsaws and spikes can make it difficult to utilize stops effectively which can result in tight and narrow confluences.

While a singular Fibonacci retracement can be meaningful on its own from time to time, two or more Fibonacci retracements or extensions that show the same thing are almost always going to lead to viable results. The concept of overlapping Fibonacci retracements is one that most traders discover on their own over time. It commonly includes the use of other types of retracements or extensions with the purpose of determining a variety of signals including support and resistance levels as well as relevant pivot points.

As such, a group of overlapping retracements is a significant improvement as two strong Fibonacci levels are all that are required in order to determine a reliable trade in many cases. Specifically, the presence of a pair of Fibonacci levels at a point of known resistance or support is almost always enough to yield viable results. The simplicity of this strategy is one of its greatest strengths and many traders use it to the exclusion of all else when trading in the forex market.

Using this strategy: When it comes to utilizing this strategy correctly, you can use any chart that you like as long as it contains either a run down or a run up of a given currency price in addition to multiple retracements. From there, you will need to begin adding Fibonacci lines to the chart. If you draw these Fibonacci lines on a powerful down trend, then you will be able to start from the high point on the chart before moving toward the lowest swing point. If you are following an uptrend, then the reverse is going to be true. Once this is done you will need to find the confluence points that comes from any Fibonacci level including 38 percent, 50 percent, 62 percent and 79 percent.

Fibonacci extensions: To use Fibonacci extensions with this strategy, the basics are going to be more or less the same. You are simply going to choose the chart of your choice before adding in the Fibonacci lines with the Fibonacci extensions enabled as well. A particularly useful time to utilize this strategy is when the market is ranging between the support and resistance levels. It doesn't matter if the actual range is long or short, it will eventually break because the market cannot stay in an indecisive position forever.

The best way to determine the direction that a ranging market is going to break in is by first determining the range on the timeframe you are considering before then determining the low and the high based on that range. If the Fibonacci levels indicate that the price is going to break above the range, then the uptrend is likely going to form and if it breaks below the range then a downtrend is likely to form. While this will allow you to more accurately determine the next major movement that is likely to occur, it is still important to wait for that instance to actually come to pass before you move to take advantage of it.

On the other hand, you may instead want to wait for the range to break out once, before getting in on the second wave. This is frequently a good idea as a vast majority of traders spend time waiting for the initial break, regardless of how far away it may be in the moment. What's more, when this does occur, the price moves a great deal in a very short period of time, causing most of these traders to close out which drops the price, which a third round of traders is then happy to take advantage of.

These first three waves typically happen quite quickly before a much larger fourth wave of traders swoops in after they finally get on board with what is actually happening. As such, the most profitable time to get in is during the third wave as you avoid paying a premium while still expecting a fair amount of the profits you would see if you managed to get in any earlier.

In order to take advantage of this movement, you are going to want to determine the initial range breakout before waiting for the price to start moving against it. You will then want to wait some more and have the price return to moving in the breakout direction once again. Once this occurs you are going to want to take the proper position and set the target to the low support line with a stop above the 0.0 level.

At this point, you will need to wait for the price to break past the lowest support line as if this does not occur then you are going to want to close out your position and try your luck again the next time the price starts following the trade in question. If the price does ultimately break through the lower support line, then you are going to wait for it to retest the broken support so that you can confidently close out your position before waiting for the price to once more come into alignment with the trend. Once it breaks past the support line but fails to crest above it, then you are going to want to take the relevant position based on the trend and set a level of 161.80 as the new target.

Assuming the trend breaks at this point and presents itself in such a way that it appears as though it is strong enough to continue to 423.60 then you will want to ensure you have the proper position and set this as your target while putting the stop loss slightly above 261.80.

Mistakes to avoid

While Fibonacci levels can provide a great deal of insight into the trading process, it can also lead to serious issues and massive losses if used incorrectly. As such, you are going to want to be aware of the following commonly made mistake sin order to ensure that your strategy works out according to plan.

Avoid mixing reference points: In order to correctly fit your retracements to the relevant price action, you are always going to want to keep steady reference points. This means that if you are using a low trend as a reference past the close of a session or in the body of a candle, then your ideal high price should always be visible in the candle at the top of the trend. Mistake and misanalysis can make it easy to accidentally skew these reference points by moving from the wick to the body of the candle hurting your potential for profit in the process. Luckily, consistently holding on to your reference points will also make it easier for you to determine accurate support and resistance levels at the moment.

Avoid ignoring long-term trends: If you get in the habit of dealing with short term charts then it can be easy to lose focus on the big picture. This narrowing of your perspective can ultimately result in misguided short-term trades if you aren't careful. Keeping a close eye on long-term trends, even if you don't plan on actively trading them can help you determine if the short-term trends you have found are all that they appear cracked up to be. Even better, this level of perception will allow you to potentially act on trends that have a great deal of momentum turning a solid 50 pip profit into one that is 400 pips or more.

CHAPTER 9: BLADERUNNER TRADING STRATEGY

The Bladerunner forex trading strategy is a type of price action strategy that utilizes price action in order to find successful entries. It also uses round numbers, resistance and support levels, candlesticks and pivot points in order to ensure its results are as accurate as possible. While it is not always going to be necessary to utilize off-chart indicators, you will also want to include your favorites if you hope to have an additional confirmation before you make your final decision. Fibonacci levels are also an option in this scenario.

Generally speaking, the best course of action is going to be to use a 20 EMA on-chart indicator or the midline of the traditional 20 Bollinger Band because either of these will properly support the strategy. Alternately, you can also use both together to further confirm that what you are seeing is correct. The results from doing so can then be traded with any currency pair along with any timeframe, though the five-minute chart is likely going to generate the best results.

While you can use this strategy successfully at any point throughout the day, there are certain times that are going to be more productive than others. For example, the early hours of the Asian session tend to generate a reasonable amount of breakout while also supplying a retest that is reliable enough to warrant entry while its later hours are typically quite slow. When it comes to the European session opens the prices are often quite volatile which makes finding an entry point a risky proposition, once things settle down it is then easier to get a few reliable entries if you are lucky.

The Bladerunner strategy got its name from the fact that the 20 EMA functions as the knife edge that divides the price. If the price ends up being higher than the EMA while at the same time respecting it and retesting the EMA then it is likely going to fall on the long side. If the price is below the EMA, while still resting and respecting, then it is likely going to end up being on the short side.

Meanwhile, if the price ends up being lower than the 20 EMA

then you will find that your basis will be short which means you will want the price to increase to the 20 EMA mark, then reject it, then turn downwards once more. Alternately, if the prices breaks through the 20 EMA and closes in a convincing fashion at a higher point you can assume the price's polarity has changed and it will now have a much longer bias. Moving forward from this point will mean waiting for a price decrease to the 20 EMA mark as the price will then reject the downward trajectory and move in a positive direction once more.

Entering properly: To setup this strategy properly you are going to want to wait for a price that breaks out of its range or consolidation pattern before choosing an entry point which is currently trending. The price you chose must successfully retest to the 20 EMA more than once before you can move forward with confidence.

In order for a retest to be considered properly successful, you are going to want to ensure the price reaches the desired EMA before going back to moving in the opposite direction. If you are looking at a candlestick chart you will see that the first candle touches the 20 EMA and closes on the side of the EMA it started from. This candle is what is known as the signal candle as the price will then bounce from the 20 EMA allowing you to wait and see if the next candle created will move in the same direction or mix things up. The candle that is created next is then known as the confirmation candle as it confirms the movement one way or the other.

Other things to keep in mind: First and foremost, if you are looking for additional confirmation before making a move, you can look for a recognizable candle pattern to confirm what the Bladerunner strategy is already telling you. While this might seem too simplistic to work properly, the fact of the matter is that these types of fundamentals will remain relevant regardless and price action is always going to need to be factored into any trading decisions you make when it comes to determining a true entry point. You will hardly ever want to make a trade based purely on the fact that you notice a rebound on the price after it hit the 20 EMA.

Additionally, you are always going to want to aim for a confluence of reasons to enter a specific trade as opposed to just banking on the rejection of the 20 EMA. This means you are going to want to wait to see the rejection and ensure that it takes place at the same point as before based on the relevant level of support or resistance. Alternately, you can also hope to find parity between the pivot point and the price impact point that relates to the currency in question.

Furthermore, you are going to want to always be aware of the likelihood that a major news announcement is going to take place during the timeframe you are focusing on for this strategy. This is particularly useful if you are planning on using long-term charts. You are going to want to avoid using this strategy up to an hour before a news release and at least 15 minutes after one is released to give the mart some time to settle down before you make your move. Doing so will make it easier for you to prevent the data from becoming skewed in a way that is extremely unreliable.

When using this strategy, you are always going to want to make a point of trading in line with the current trend based on whatever side of the 20 EMA the price came down on.

Placing orders

While the parameters outlined below recommend spreading each entry across two orders, one order and one position per trade is also effective. However, two positions are often preferable as it will provide you with a greater level of flexibility when it comes to exiting the trade in a profitable position.

Long entry: For a long entry you are going to want to start by placing a pair a pair of stop orders to buy at an entry point 2 pips above the point that was confirmed by the confirmatory candle. These orders should be set to expire at the start of the next candle window. For example, if you started on the five-minute chart then your stop orders would expire when the next five-minute candle started. The exception to this rule being if they end up being terminated due to price action before the next candle has a chance to form. The profit takeaway from the first order will be a set amount equal to the risk inherent in the pips you chose. The profit takeaway from the second order would then be a set amount equal to double the inherent risk in its pips.

Short entry: In order to set up a short entry successfully, you are going to being by placing a pair of sell stop order with an open entry point that is 2 pips below the point the confirmatory candle indicated. These orders should be set to expire at the start of the next candle. For example, if you started on the five-minute chart then your stop orders would expire when the next five-minute candle started. The exception to this rule being if they end up being terminated due to price action before the next candle has a chance to form.

From there, you will want to place the stop loss at a point that is 2 pips above the point where the signal candle first met the 20 EMA. Don't forget, this is just a general guideline and you may also want to place the stop at a point above the swing point to ensure a stop that is properly realistic. Finally, the profit takeaway from the first order will be a set amount equal to the risk inherent in the pips you chose. The profit takeaway from the second order would then be a set amount equal to double the inherent risk in its pips.

Stop trailing: Once the price has finished moving in the direction you were expecting by the amount equal to the amount of its initial risk, then one of the orders you place will close after it reaches the anticipated amount of profit. The second order will then be moved to a breakeven scenario. The second order will then be left near the breakeven point until the market closes out the trade via stopping out at the breakeven point or possibly reaching the target profit amount. If you know another announcement is forthcoming, then the best course of action at this point is to allow it to continue to trail beyond the breakeven point, assuming you expect the news to break in your favor.

Polarity indicator: In order to use this strategy as effectively as possible, you may want to use the forex polarity indicator in addition to your other favorite indicators. In this situation, you will find that you will use it in much the same way you would a mid-Bollinger Band, or even the 20 EMA. The polarity indicator combines these two indicators which are often used in the major trading houses where the price influences are felt more keenly.

In order to utilize this indicator to the fullest, you will want to start by plotting out the polarity indicator as a means of establishing a trend as in addition to any relevant biases. If you find the price trading at a point that is above the polarity indicator, then the trend can be considered bullish and if it is currently trading at a point that is above the polarity indicator, then it is bearish. Regardless, you will want to wait for the price to break past the dominant position. Once this occurs, you will then wait for the return before using the resulting candlestick to retest the polarity indicator one more time.

The ribbon that is created when you utilize both indicators will provide you with additional detail about the movement and help you guard against false positives. Furthermore, doing so will allow you to determine if a signal that you take to be week is actually strong enough to base a trade around. Using both indicators at the same time is an effective way to continue making profitable trades even if you find the price to be stuck within a less than ideal range over a prolonged period of time as it clears out all of the false signals.

If you use both indicators, then they typically provide you with a zone you can count on to cause the price to react. If the price stops below this signal zone, then it will typically reject and move back to the short side after it enters and if it dips down to the zone then you can expect it to slowly come back down before retesting in the area that is bounded by the pair of indicators before ultimately going back up once again.

Bladerunner reversal

The Bladerunner reversal strategy is a useful way to successfully tackle a crossover strategy. A variation of such also uses the polarity indicator as well as the 20EMA or the Bollinger mid-band. Keep in mind, however, that if you do use the polarity indicator you will not see the standard cross as it is likely to only become apparent if you first analyze the yellow band that you will notice expanding and contracting, assuming you use the mid-Bollinger band and the 20 EMA at the same time.

The biggest difference with the reversal variation of this strategy comes from the fact that it trades based on the crossover of the two indicators. Specifically, the Bladerunner prime strategy encourages you to wait out a confirmed trend before trading the bounces opposite the direction the trend is moving. However, the reversal comes into play once the trend is already up and running and the price is ready and willing to reverse in order to close on the far side of the same polarity indicator. Both of these strategies still trade in the direction the trend indicates as determined by the closing price on the side of the polarity indicator that benefits either the short or long call depending.

The pattern that you are seeking out in this instance is for the price to break out of the channel and then trend with significant strength in a single direction. It will then stall and reverse course before passing through the polarity indicator and coming back to retest the chosen indicator from the opposite direction. For example, consider a scenario where, during the Asian session, the price is going to decrease until it breaks through the weekly pivot point before stalling and reversing at the nearest round number. The price could then easily form another indecisive band for the entirety of the remainder of the Asian session before seeing yet another surge below the point of the polarity indicator.

The result of all of this is that the price jumps from the round number only to ultimately close on the far side of the polarity indicator. After this occurs, the mid-Bollinger band and the 20 EMA will have both crossed over, giving you a stronger crossover signal. Furthermore, you will also need to keep an eye on the engulfing candlestick pattern as if it is bullish then this signals a strong possibility of a future entry point based on either a secondary bullish engulfing candlestick assuming it close above the current range or presents as a morning-star pattern.

This example will only work if you have a bullish perspective on the market as a whole. Alternately, if you were bearish on the state of the market then you would use the same strategy, you would just approach the trade from the opposite direction. This would mean that an upward move would need to be completed before the price can successfully break though in order to return back the way it came multiple times. Each time it should crest beneath the polarity indicator and create an evening star pattern instead.

Utilizing both the Bladerunner reversal and the standard Bladerunner strategy in the same session is a great way to accurately cope with a price that is not trending in a single direction for any prolonged period of time. Doing so effectively creates a reliable EMA scalping strategy.

CHAPTER 10: TIPS FOR SHORTENING YOUR TRADING WORK WEEK

Early on in your new trading career, you are going to have to accept the fact that you are going to need to work harder than the traders who have been in the game longer in order to achieve the same results. It is only natural, after all, as you have to put far more time into covering the basics while they only need to check in on the things that change from week to week. As such, as you become more proficient at trading in the forex market you will find that you are able to naturally do more with less. The following tips and tricks will help ensure you get to that point as quickly as possible.

Be aware of overtrading: First things first, even if you are just getting started, it is important to understand that sometimes the best way to win is not to play. Simply put, if you feel the available selection, or market as a whole, is poor, then the best option is going to likely be holding out and waiting for things to improve before you waste time working towards a suboptimal goal. Time and time again, undisciplined and hyperactive investors run their portfolios into the ground by increasing their costs, decreasing their tax benefits and missing the natural action of the stock markets. Getting a grip on how often they pull the trigger is crucial in keeping their portfolio moving in a positive direction.

The simple fact of the matter is that even if you are staying away from the worst of the worst trading scenarios the odds are still fairly high that you are trading more frequently than the pros. In fact, if most professionals traded as frequently as the average private trader then they would lose their jobs. Keep in mind that the service fee you pay on a commission can seriously cut into your overall profits, especially if they happen far more often than they should. As a general rule, you should aim to limit your trading costs to between one and two percent of your total portfolio if you are aiming for returns that rest firmly in the double digits.

Understand the spread: In addition to trading costs, may traders that are overtrading aren't taking the bid-ask spread into account properly. As there are very few limitations when it comes to the forex market, the spread you might find in some scenarios could be dramatically skewed against you, and this is something that you will need to keep in mind if you want to keep your profits in tip top shape. Even if you aren't spending all that much per trade, at face value, you could easily end up spend about five percent of the cost of the trade on a spread, which can really add up over a year or more.

Taxes: Assuming you are good (and lucky) enough to pull off a profitable year trading in the forex market, then it is going to eventually be time to pay taxes on your good fortune. Unfortunately, if you are very good (or very lucky) and make a fair amount of profit, this can push you into a higher tax bracket which is why it is important to handle your profits carefully. Making more while working less is all about holding onto as much of your money as possible, including during tax time.

Consider slow turnover: It's not just that heavy trading can take its toll on a portfolio; it's that the absence of lower turnover can also rob a portfolio of valuable components. Trying to follow every up-and-down tick of your favorite currency pairs, plus all the news headlines that could affect them, can leave many investors feeling a little strung out. As a consequence of being overloaded, many investors' psychology becomes more erratic, and they make investment choices on adrenaline and impulse. Trying to time trades distracts many investors from doing critical research.

Regardless of the type of trader you are, it is important to not let over trading get in your way, and if you started off trading more than you should, ween yourself off this crutch as soon as possible. In fact, the odds are good that if you lower your turnover rate and spend the time you used to spend trading doing research, then the trades you do end up making are naturally going to be more effective as a result.

Generally speaking, one of the biggest missed opportunities when it comes to maintaining a high-turnover portfolio comes from missing out on guaranteed profits that come along with regular interest payments. In fact, some studies estimate that interest payments account for as much as half of the overall long-term growth.

Overtrading alternatives

Diversify: Regardless of your motivations, there are almost always going to be more effective ways of trading than by overtrading on a regular basis. If you do prefer to micromanage your trades, one of the first things you are going to want to do is to diversify the currency pairs you are holding as not focusing all of your energy around a single currency pair will naturally lead to less micromanagement as you don't have to worry about one bad trade completely wiping out your trading capital.

Even if you find that you are making approximately the same number of trades on the surface, the amount of work required will be lower, decreasing the overall amount of time spent as a result. You are also far less likely to make any trading mistakes, as you will be making fewer trades, improving your overall results in the process.

Get someone else to do it for you: Of course, one way to decidedly shorten the amount of time you need to put into the process is to find someone else to manage your trading capital for you. You can still tell them what type of strategies you prefer as well as what your short and long-term goals are, but then you will be able to sit back and watch as they do all of the heavy lifting. You aren't going to be able to buy into these types of services cheap, however, as you will need to have a minimum of $50,000 in available trading capital to apply for most privately managed forex accounts.

Be realistic: The fact of the matter is that in order to be a successful, active, trader you need to be willing to dedicate a large portion of your waking life to the enterprise. Not only that, but if you can't remain on your game at all times then you are likely going to end up with a loss when everything is said and done no matter how rapidly you trade. If you don't have the ability to trade at the highest level, then you will almost always find more success by taking a more measured, less time-intensive approach to trading.

Consider the long-term: While taking a short-term approach to forex trading can result in some decent returns in decent timeframe, if you aren't planning on doing much with your profits at the moment, then taking a long-term approach will not only cut down on the amount of work you need to do regularly, it will likely benefit you far more down the line.

Essentially, when you reinvest your early profits back into the market, you stand to make quite a bit more in the long-term, especially if you have a timeline that accounts for decades of potential growth. Reinvesting both early and regularly is crucial when it comes to maximizing your profits in both the short and the long-term.

To understand what compounding can really do, picture a 25-year-old who is looking to be a millionaire by the time they retire. In order to do so, they will need to save $900 each month for 40 years, assuming they see a poor 5 percent yearly return on their investment. However, if they wait 10 years to get started then they are going to need to save about $2,000 a month for the next 30 years to get to the same point. Furthermore, if they waited 20 years they would need to save $4,000 a month to reach the same point.

In addition to getting started as quickly as possible, it is also important that you understand your personal investment habits in order to ensure that you are helping, rather than hindering, your investments. Don't forget, no strategy is going to be the right choice for everyone, and it all comes down to how comfortable with risk you are.

You are also going to want to consider your goals when it comes to investing as these can easily affect the outcome of the strategy that you ultimately choose. This could be something reliable, such as ensuring that your initial investment isn't lost no matter what, or it could be something a good deal riskier, counting on the larger risk to lead to greater rewards more often than not. The specifics themselves aren't as important as the fact that once you set a plan you make the decision to stick with it no matter what. When it comes to making your plan, don't forget it doesn't take place in a vacuum which means you may have numerous different external factors to consider as well.

Consider your research

Regardless if you prefer fundamental or technical analysis, you have likely gotten used to doing far more research than you do actual trading. After all, regardless of what indicators or trends you favor, it seems as though there is always something new to investigate further. Unfortunately, until things play out, there is no guarantee that the research you are doing is actually going to produce any positive results, ensuring that every minute spent researching is naturally infused with a little bit of risk. After all, regardless of the direction a given currency pair is expected to move, it can spin the opposite direction with little notice.

Research often builds in a directional bias as well. This can mean that a trader will only trade in one direction based on his or her research, even when price indicates the opposite. While it is prudent to "trade with the trend," only looking at one side of the market can lead to missed opportunities or, even worse, failure to realize when we are on the wrong side of a trade.

Luckily, if you stick to short-term trades you will have a greater ability to react in a nimble fashion, moving in and out of positions as the market demands. As such, doing too much research can actually tie you too closely to a given course of action, making you less nimble in the process.

Trying something else: One alternative to the level of research you will likely find yourself doing a lot of as a novice forex trader is to instead look into the currency pairs that are going to be most likely to be tradable every day based on their daily statistics. As such, if you cast a broader net, and watch a number of potential options, when one of them pops, you will still be ready to maximize your profits as thoroughly as possible. What's more, you also eliminate directional bias as you are able to move in multiple directions depending on how the market ultimately shakes out.

To decrease your workload even more, you could work from a longer timeframe so that you only have to do your research once a week, or even once a month to remain moderately competitive. Depending on the types of trades that you are interested in, you should be able to set the screen to look for small and consistent movement just as easily as large, slower options as well.

Time sinks to avoid

Not using the 80-20 rule: The 80:20 rule states that 80 percent of the results you see from trading should come from 20 percent of your actions. While this is easy to say, many traders don't fully understand what parts of the trading process should be emphasized and what should be kicked to the curb. Generally speaking, you are going to find better results if you spend your time doing things like reviewing your performance and creating guidelines based around it that match your trading strategy. You will also want to spend time curating your watchlist of viable currencies, ensuring you have a quality price alerts set up and journal regarding your success and your failures.

You are going to want to keep detailed notes related to all the trades you make to help you determine personal patterns that otherwise may not be visible. This means you are going to want to keep track of not just success and failures, but how given trades were determined and your emotional state throughout. Once you have enough examples to see the patterns you will want to strengthen the positive ones through conscious usage and do your best to minimize the negatives.

Meanwhile, you are also going to want to avoid doing things like switching timeframes and currency pairs too frequently or watching your trades as they move pip by pip. Additionally, while you may find viable strategies from talking to other traders online, you will only waste time by getting into social media wars or hoping on every new trading method that comes along. Now many of these things are going to be habits you pick up in the early days of forex trading, and that is to be expected. As long as you are aware of the things you are doing and take the right steps to ween them out of your daily trading habits then you are well on your way to shortening your trading work week substantially.

Not getting away from micromanaging: While early on there are likely plenty of viable reasons for you to micromanage your trades, in order to successfully cut your trading time down to just 30 minutes per day, you are going to need to actively work to avoid this practice. In addition to frequently leading to a wide variety of mistakes as they watch their trades move pip by pip, many new traders waste time doing things like second guessing themselves by moving stop losses around or looking for additional confirmation from third parties. Both of these add nothing productive to the process and only increase the likelihood that mistakes are made by adding more cooks to the kitchen.

Another serious issue that this type of activity often brings about is changes to the trading plan that are made in the moment. Now there is certainly a time and a place for improvisation, in the middle of a trade that is going well, for no other reason than because you were bored is certainly not one of them. Trading successfully is all about being able to stick to a plan in a way that is reliable enough to be counted on no matter what, the fact that it also means you don't have to spend countless hours micromanaging each and every trade is just an added bonus.

To avoid these mistakes, you are going to want to work towards making more trades of the "set it and forget it" variety. By seeking out trades that are as low-volatility as possible, you will be able to set your limits when it comes to profits and losses, and then not have to worry about looking at your trades again, except to check in once and a while to ensure that things are proceeding according to plan. After all, the price of the currencies is going to do whatever it is that they are going to do which means that there is very little for you to actually do assuming you proceeded correctly up to this point.

This sort of approach has the potential to not only improve the quality of one's trading, but it also boosts the performance when traders stop micro-managing their trades. The main reason why traders can't stop this habit is because they don't trust their system, they only think about the money involved, they haven't validated their edge or don't have any trading rules at all. Once you are ready to start actively thinking about minimizing your time spent trading, you are also ready to start trusting yourself. Stop worrying about keeping a close eye on everything, it is time to learn to trust yourself and your system.

Not fighting boredom: Another common mistake that many new traders make is not taking into account that large swaths of trading are extremely boring, and micromanaging your trades is even more so. Not taking this boredom into account early on can easily lead to an increase in mistakes that stem from a desire to do something, regardless of the results, just to watch something happen.

Needless to say, boredom is an extremely dangerous emotion and will lead to nothing but poor trading decisions if not kept in check. Luckily, as you make an active effort to cut down on inessential trading time you should find that you are naturally spending less time staring at a screen, so the problem should solve itself.

Not choosing the right trades: A successful trade is always going to be built on a measured approach. To ensure this is the case you are going to want to begin by choosing the type of forex pairs that align with your goals as well as your temperament. Furthermore, you are going to want to take any external knowledge you might have into account when choosing the pairs to focus on. Regardless, it is important to always take the following three main aspects of every trade into account before you make any decisions.

First and foremost, you are always going to want to trade in a timeframe that you are comfortable with. Doing otherwise will simply lead to scenarios where you are not at your best because you are impatient or just plain nervous. While you were still trying to improve your overall trade percentage, you likely tried to stick to the shorter charts to help you become truly comfortable dealing with the potential for risk that holding pairs for longer timeframes can cause. That time has passed, however, and now you should focus on longer timeframes, bigger payoffs, and less work.

When it comes to choosing a methodology to use while trading it is important to focus on what works for you instead of bouncing around based on what is popular in the moment. It is important to remember that every trader is going to have good days and bad days and if you can find a methodology that is successful at least 60 percent of the time then you are well on your way to success. Switching your tactics constantly is only going to skew your stats so you won't be able to determine the true cause of either your successes or your failures. What's worse, changing constantly will make it difficult for you to learn the intricacies of the methodologies you use meaning they will be less effective in even more scenarios.

CONCLUSION

Thank you for making it through to the end of *Forex: Proven Forex Trading Money Making Strategy – Just 30 Minutes a Day*, let's hope it was informative and able to provide you with all of the tools you need to achieve your goals, whatever it is that they may be. Just because you've finished this book doesn't mean there is nothing left to learn on the topic, expanding your horizons is the only way to find the mastery you seek.

Specifically, if you are dedicated to the idea of making the most money possible from the forex market while putting in as little day-to-day work as possible, then you are always going to be on the lookout for additional ways to streamline the experience. Whether this is by improving the way in which you determine your trades, removing your bad habits from the equation, researching more efficiently or some combination of the three, the only way to ever improve is through hard work and dedication.

While early on it will likely feel as though there is nothing you can do to ensure you trade as effectively as possible, with time you will learn where your strengths and weakness lie, as well as what you can do to correct them. Don't expect this understanding to come overnight, however, as you will only learn where you can improve after plenty of trial and error has taken place. If you start out trying to minimize your time right from the start, you won't get anywhere, you have to have a basic understanding of the process before you can ever hope to improve. Always remember, learning to find success without spending all day trading in the forex market is a marathon, not a sprint, which means slow and steady wins the race.

Finally, if you found this book useful in any way, a review on Amazon is always appreciated!

Made in the USA
Middletown, DE
17 August 2019